T0196038

# WHY IS IT SO DIFFICULT TO FORGIVE FROM A BIBLICAL PERSPECTIVE?

Robert E. Gaines Sr., PhD

WESTBOW
PRESS®
A DIVISION OF THOMAS NELSON
& ZONDERVAN

WestBow Press books may be ordered through booksellers or by contacting:

WestBow Press
A Division of Thomas Nelson & Zondervan
1663 Liberty Drive
Bloomington, IN 47403
www.westbowpress.com
844-714-3454

ISBN: 978-1-6642-0453-9 (sc)
ISBN: 978-1-6642-0452-2 (hc)
ISBN: 978-1-6642-0454-6 (e)

Library of Congress Control Number: 2020916979

Print information available on the last page.

WestBow Press rev. date: 09/21/2020

This project is dedicated first to my Lord and Savior Jesus Christ who laid his life down for me and rose for my justification. It is because of him that I have something to share about forgiveness after being forgiven and to my wife, Crystal Gaines, and our kids, Robert Gaines Jr., Braylen Gaines, and Amari Gaines. It would not have been possible without their sacrifice.

I also thank my mother-in-law, Oretha Whitley, for the many days she volunteered to keep the kids to give me time to study and complete assignments.

I would like to thank my mother, Ruthie Gaines, for loving me unconditionally through the years, and for the many sacrifices she has made for me and our family. She has been an exceptional mother and a caregiver for so many.

I thank my father for the principles he taught me early in life about being a man. Thank you for being firm with me when needed and loving to show me that men can be strong and loving. Thank you, Dad, for teaching me that a man's word is his bond. Thank you for showing me that hard work will pay off.

I want to thank my brother, David, for making sure I did not become a victim of the streets at a young age. I am grateful that God blessed me to have a brother, and I love you.

I also want to thank many of the special people who have helped me behind the scenes. I will not call out your names out of respect for your wishes to not be listed. Thank you for encouraging me to finish. Without you, it would not have been possible.

Last but certainly not least, I thank God for sending me to the St. Mark Baptist Church of Morehouse in Bonita, Louisiana. God, through the St. Mark Baptist Church, has done more for me than words can describe. I am grateful to the entire church family. Special thanks to Prince Whitmore for your love and support through the years in various capacities. Thank you, John Washington, Debra Washington and the Washington family, for all you do behind the scenes and for becoming one of my biggest supporters. I love you all so much and thank God for our church family daily. Thank God for everyone who helped in this process but I did not name specifically. I am grateful for your support.

# CONTENTS

# INTRODUCTION

When Jesus asked his disciples to forgive their trespassers so that God would also forgive them, he was teaching them one of the most important yet controversial lessons ever. They were amazed at what was required of them by Jesus, and some of them did not take it lightly. A typical example in this regard is Peter and his struggles to accept the message of forgiveness as handed down by Jesus. He eventually overcame his caution and asked Jesus a straightforward and specific question on forgiveness:

> Then came Peter to him, and said, "Lord, how oft shall my brother sin against me, and I forgive him? Till seven times?" Jesus saith unto him, "I say not unto thee, until seven times: but, until seventy times seven."[1]

Peter's question illustrates the fact that forgiving is not an easy thing. At the very least, Peter must have expected that forgiveness had to be done just for several times; after that, it was no longer necessary. By using the number seven as his supposed maximum times for forgiving, Peter must have found forgiving to be quite hard—or even impossible. He must have expected Jesus to approve him by agreeing with his time frame within which forgiveness would be given. Without going into the debates surrounding Jesus's answer, the answer illustrates that forgiveness has to be virtually limitless, unlike what people were proposing or thinking. The very fact that his response made the disciples quite concerned means that forgiveness is one act that is extremely hard to accomplish or undertake.

This lesson taught by Jesus on forgiveness shows that while forgiving is hard for human beings, it is not as hard to God. Forgiveness takes place within one's heart when the offended person makes the conscious decision

---

[1] Matthew 18:21–22 KJV.

to release the offender. Forgiveness is usually releasing from the expectation the offender will ever be able to make right the harm or hurt caused to the offended person. Forgiveness also takes place when the angry person ceases identifying the offender by their offense. However, human beings find forgiveness to be hard to accomplish.

Yet this is not what God expects human beings to do. He particularly expects those who have been called by him to forgive even as we have been forgiven or plans to be forgiven.[2] Jesus says, "For if ye forgive men their trespasses, your heavenly Father will also forgive you: But if ye forgive not men their trespasses, neither will your Father forgive your trespasses."[3] Then he goes ahead and says that a neighbor should be forgiven seventy times seven. This message by Jesus means that it has to be without any limitations or conditions. Yet the very fact that his disciples asked the questions means that even for them, forgiveness was a major hurdle that they often unsuccessfully tried to overcome. To date, Christians and non-Christians alike struggle to forgive those who offend them and instead look for different reasons to justify their not being able to forgive or why forgiving the offender is not just appropriate or warranted.

On the other hand, though, one of God's most significant acts of love for his people is demonstrated through forgiveness. God was the first to forgive—and he forgave the entire world—when he chose to overlook their sins and instead have his Son die on the cross for the atonement of the sins. Through Jesus Christ's suffering and death on Calvary's cross, all of humanity received redemption for sin. No longer are human beings required to bear the cost of their sins because Jesus bore them on their behalf. He took our iniquities and nailed them on the cross so that those who believe in him should never have to perish as a result of their sins but have eternal life.

In the same way, Jesus demonstrated an eagerness to forgive all those who wronged him. Going against the law of the Jews requiring that those who broke the Mosaic law should be punished, Jesus showed that lack of forgiveness was not to be something believers embraced and practiced.

---

[2] June Hunt, *Biblical Counseling Keys on Forgiveness: The Freedom to Let Go* (Dallas, TX: Hope for the Heart, 2008), 34.
[3] Matthew 6:14–15 KJV.

Instead, they had to readily forgive because, as he put it, everyone has sinned and falls short of the glory of God. In the incident of the woman who had been caught committing adultery and was on the verge of being stoned by the mob, Jesus sought to know from the accusers if there was anyone among them who was without any sin ever. Because all of them had sinned, no one threw a stone at the woman, and Jesus also pardoned her. This particular story demonstrates two opposing forces with Jesus on one side—the side of forgiveness—and the Jewish leadership and public on the other—the side of not forgiving.

Therefore, it is clear that the process of forgiveness is often complicated. Forgiving others may be a simple matter for some, and it may be a struggle for others. It is in humanity's fallen nature to hold on to resentment, broken relationships, and unresolved conflicts. God wants his people to follow in his steps and walk the road of forgiveness that leads to blessing and freedom. God's desire for us to walk in his footsteps leads to the ultimate question and one that deserves answering: why is it so hard to forgive? The main focus of this book is to use the Bible as the source of truth in seeking to answer this question and to address the entire topic. The biblical text has the answers to the question about forgiveness. As has just been noted, different views exist on the subject of forgiveness or the lack of forgiveness. However, most of the available discussions are not based on the truths of the Holy Scriptures but on the views of human beings who themselves struggle to forgive.

While some of these scholarly views on why forgiveness is difficult may make a lot of sense, they do not necessarily represent biblical truth. Instead, the only source of such truth is the Bible. Forgiveness is deemed a vital subject matter and one worth investigating in this book because it points to an essential part of the Gospel message. Christ spent significant amounts of his time teaching his disciples on the need for them to forgive others. Therefore, it is essential to understand what forgiveness means or entails—as well as what it is not. The truth of the matter is that at one point or another, all human beings, especially Christians, have needed to forgive or will need to forgive. Similarly, everyone will need to be forgiven. That is almost guaranteed given humanity's nature to offend one another during their relationships and interactions.

This book is a journey through the scriptures to discover why it is so hard to forgive and what can be done to accomplish it from a biblical perspective. The book is divided into several chapters, each of which contributes to the achievement of the overall research objective. Chapter 1 focuses on the misconceptions of forgiveness, and the second chapter discusses the meaning of forgiveness. The third chapter discusses the Christian motivation to forgive, and the fourth chapter focuses on understanding the freedom found in forgiveness. In the fifth chapter, the discussion moves to the process of forgiveness, and the sixth chapter explains the benefits of completing the process of forgiving.

# CHAPTER 1

# THE MISCONCEPTIONS OF FORGIVENESS

It is essential to point out that everyone has had a tough time trying to forgive people who have wronged them since the beginning of time.[4] If people were asked to provide a genuine reason why they thought forgiving the other person was hard or impossible, a variety of answers would no doubt be given. However, it is almost certain that most of the answers given would be based on preexisting misconceptions of forgiveness. One of the primary reasons why people find, or regard, forgiveness as difficult is that they have deeply entrenched misconceptions about forgiving. In this chapter, some of the common misconceptions about forgiveness are presented and discussed.

## Forgiving Helps the Other Person

Perhaps one of the most common misconceptions about forgiveness is that forgiving is essential or helpful to the other person. This form of thinking has prevented many people from forgiving those who have wronged them because they keep believing or hoping that the longer they do not forgive the person, the more the person hurts. This explains why people will repeatedly talk about how much they were hurt by the person and how they cannot think of forgiving the person.[5] This statement contains a

---

[4] June Hunt, *Biblical Counseling Keys on Forgiveness: The Freedom to Let Go* (Dallas, TX: Hope for the Heart, 2008), 39.

[5] Everett L. Worthington Jr., *Handbook of Forgiveness* (Abingdon, United Kingdom: Routledge, 2007), 26.

significant misconception about forgiveness. This statement seems to imply that the deeper an individual has hurt a person, the less the need for forgiveness. It promotes a belief that deep hurts are to be repaid through not forgiving—perhaps so that the individual can also suffer.

In reality, though, the offending individual does not suffer in any way from a person's refusal to forgive. Instead, the person who refuses to forgive is the one who suffers. It may be argued that people who choose not to forgive may bear two different burdens in their hearts: the weight of having been hurt so deeply and the preoccupation of thinking what the offender is up to or thinking about the situation. Most—if not all—of the time, the offending person has long forgotten the incident. At times, the offender is not even aware that he or she offended someone or that that person might be hurting deeply.

Therefore, choosing to forgive has the added advantage of helping the offender come to the realization of the mistake they may have inadvertently committed. Because the offender has no idea of the crime, or has long forgotten about it, there is usually almost no way the offender is going to be hurt by the offense. Because it has been forgotten, it leaves the offended party as the only person who holds the hurt and continually replays it in his or her mind to reaffirm its severity and justify the decision not to forgive. The offended party is also the one who falsely believes that the offender is the one hurting.

True forgiveness hardly ever comes until the offended person makes two important discoveries. The first is that failure to forgive is akin to keeping somebody in prison, and the second is that the person who is incarcerated is the offended. Refusal to forgive is not like an ordinary prison; it is one where individuals willingly lock themselves in based on false beliefs. There is reason to believe that every offended human being, by nature of our fallen state, would wish for the offender to come to some form of harm or to suffer immensely so that the offense can be atoned for. This thinking is part of the reason why people refuse to forgive and instead keep replaying the battery and the subsequent hurt over and over in their minds.

Offended people choose not to let go because they think that letting go allows the offender to get away with the offense. They want the offender to pay for the offense by suffering equal (if not worse) pain as they suffered or are suffering. The offender is never affected in any way by a lack of forgiveness. Instead, failure to forgive hurts the offended party even more; this is why a lack of forgiveness is considered a self-imposed prison. Jesus used one specific parable to show that those who do not forgive deserve to be put into a physical prison (like the unmerciful servant). Jesus says, "So likewise shall my heavenly Father do also unto you if ye from your hearts forgive not every one his brother their trespasses."[6] This is the only kind of prison where prisoners have all the powers to do whatever they please, including the ability to leave jail and never return. However, prisoners also have the potential to come back if and when they desire.

The latter is an essential issue because many times offended people have chosen to forgive someone but then never went all the way—they thought of forgiving but never really forgave. This principle is akin to walking about in a self-imposed prison without really getting out—even though the prisoner has the prison cell key and knows where the door out of jail is. In essence, the prisoner knows and understands all there is to know and understand to be free. However, he or she chooses not to let himself or herself out of the prison because he or she is somewhat convinced that doing so would be freeing the offender from prison. This idea is one of the worst misconceptions because the offender is in no jail at all. The person who is in prison—the one who is hurting and bearing the emotional and mental consequences of the suffering—is the offended person. Unless and until the angry person chooses to forgive without any conditions, he or she may never realize that he or she is in a self-made prison.

One of the best examples of true forgiveness is Jesus Christ, who, after all the suffering and subsequent crucifixion, was made to die on the cross by the Jewish religious leaders. Jesus still had the sense of mind to ask his Father to forgive his persecutors:

---

[6] Valary, Anthony. "We Must Forgive." Praise Houston. Praise Houston, July 2, 2019. https://praisehouston.com/4052921/we-must-forgive/. "Matthew 18:35 KJV: "So Likewise Shall My Heavenly Father Do Also unto You, If Ye from Your Hearts Forgive Not Every One His..." Matthew 18:35 KJV "So likewise shall my heavenly Father do also unto you, if ye from your hearts forgive not every one his...". Accessed December 12, 2019. https://www.kingjamesbibleonline.org/Matthew-18-35/.

Then said Jesus, Father, forgive them; for they know not what they do. And they parted his raiment and cast lots.[7]

The question worth asking at this point is: Why did Jesus ask for his killers to be forgiven by God? The answer could be found in the fact that Jesus did not have the same misconception about forgiveness. Instead, he knew that he needed to unconditionally forgive them for his benefit. Jesus benefitted from forgiving his killers in that his prayers would not be hindered. For it is written:

And when ye stand praying, forgive, if ye have ought against any: that your Father also which is in heaven may forgive you your trespasses. But if ye do not forgive, neither will your Father which is in heaven forgive your trespasses.[8]

Had Jesus's prayers to the Father been hindered as a result of not forgiving, his mission on earth would possibly not have been accomplished. This is because refusing to forgive would have compelled his Father in heaven not to listen to him or hear his prayers and supplications.[9] By forgiving, a whole new world of possibilities was opened up before Jesus. Forgiveness helped him continue being in constant and unhindered communion with his Father through prayer,[10] something that would have become impossible if he had chosen not to forgive.

Jesus's persecutors never really cared about what happened to him or its implications. Most of them were never aware that they had done anything wrong by crucifying the Messiah. Instead, they understood that they had done a great favor to people by ridding them of someone who posed an existential threat to Rome's rule and who allegedly blasphemed

[7] "Then Jesus said, 'Father, forgive them, for they do not know what they are doing.' And they divided up His garments by casting lots." Accessed December 15, 2019. https://biblehub.com/luke/23-34.htm.

[8] Mark 11:25–26 KJV.

[9] John 11:42 KJV. In this verse, Jesus says, "And I knew that thou hearest me always: but because of the people which stand by I said it, that they may believe that thou hast sent me."

[10] John 14:16 KJV.

God by claiming equality with God.[11] There were no direct or immediate consequences for them.

Therefore, refusal to forgive hurts not the offending but the offended person. The implication is that forgiveness is usually hard to come by because the offended party—who has all the power and decision-making necessary for forgiveness to take place—is generally trying to achieve something virtually impossible: hurt the other party. As long as offended people think that their offender is the one who is injured (or most hurt) when forgiveness is withheld, then forgiveness will continue to be withheld. However, the realization that failure to forgive only hurts the offended party more could make forgiving easier to do.

There is a reason to believe that no person will be willing to keep oneself in jail for a moment longer. This is if one realizes that he or she has all the keys out of prison. Also, the person will be quite unhappy with oneself for having been foolish enough not to realize that he or she had the key to the jail all along. They may be more annoyed at themselves for understanding that no one really brought them to the prison and that they willingly brought themselves into the prison, locked themselves up, and rejected any attempts by well-wishers to let themselves out. While this may sound like a fairy tale, it depicts the situation in which an offended person finds oneself when he or she refuses to forgive.

Having noted that, it is essential to add that there is no doubt that the offended person suffers a lot as a result of having been offended. This is not something that anyone can minimize. However, the hurt that comes from the refusal to forgive is often more severe—and its effects are more debilitating—than the damage that results from the actual offense. This is why the decision to forgive ends the emotional and mental suffering of the offended party and not of the offender. If every angry person had the patience and wisdom to understand that refusal to forgive would only add to the hurt caused by the offense to oneself and not to the offender, they would readily forgive. Subsequently, forgiveness would never have to be so hard to come by or accomplish. If not for anything else, offended people would be willing to forgive not to magnify their hurt and harm caused by the offense.

---

[11] John 10:33 KJV.

Refusal to forgive is also likened to the offended person's consumption of poison but with the expectation that it is the offender who will be harmed by the poison. The Bible may not directly use the word "poison" (as it has directly used the word "prison"), but it still makes it clear that forgiveness is not suitable for the bones or that it brings about healing.

> But to you who fear My name the Sun of Righteousness shall arise with healing in His wings; and you shall go out and grow fat like stall-fed calves.[12]

> A merry heart doeth good *like* a medicine: but a broken spirit drieth the bones.[13]

In Malachi, those who fear God's name are brought together with those who are arrogant and have no fear of the Lord. It is such people (especially the arrogant) who fail to forgive because the proud cannot forgive. In Proverbs, the broken spirit being mentioned is similar to that of a person who does not forgive. One of the most frequent manifestations of lack of forgiveness is a heart that is devoid of joy, a spirit that is broken. Such a person's health slowly wastes away. However, when the person chooses to forgive, the release results in a kind of healing that is similar to that brought about by taking medicine. Therefore, forgiving is like medicine to the heart.

It is absurd for a person to consume poison and then expect that their offender will be harmed by the poison. In reality, the person who takes the poison is the one who is damaged by it. More often than not, the consumption of poison leads to death. Refusing to forgive may not lead to death—at least not in the short term or even medium term—but its effects are usually long term and debilitating to the extent that they may hasten one's actual death. The bitterness and resentment that a person harbors have been known to eat at someone gradually over time. As this happens, the offender has no idea of the suffering of the offended person and goes about one's daily activities as though nothing happened. Since

---

[12] Malachi 4:2 NIV.
[13] Proverbs 17:22 KJV.

the offender is not aware, this goes to underscore the fact that refusal to forgive hardly ever—if at all—harms the offender but certainly harms the offended person.

One of the most critical issues regarding forgiveness is that it helps the offended person and not the offender overcome the hurt and not have to live with the burden of not forgiving. This is because not forgiving is choosing to live with a burden in one's heart. This is a burden that—like all burdens—weights down a person slowly and has other effects. People who do not forgive or who hold onto resentment, anger, bitterness, and rage have been known to live shorter lives than people who readily forgive and quickly let go of their pent-up anger, resentment, rage, and bitterness.

The verse in Malachi sums it up quite well by saying that when the heart is merry, it does "good" like medicine. People who are continually happy hardly ever suffer from common sicknesses because of happiness—or a cheerful heart for that matter—has been proven to cause the body to produce certain hormones that fight pathogens. This happens because these hormones strengthen the body's immune system by encouraging the production of white blood cells responsible for fighting disease-causing organisms.

On the contrary, a heart that is sad, sullen, and without happiness encourages the body to produce large amounts of hormones that weaken rather than strengthen the immune system. A common manifestation of this is usually in the form of stomach ulcers, which are closely associated with unhappiness. These ulcers are more likely to develop among sad people than happy people. Moreover, the ability of stomach ulcers to heal significantly depends on the emotional health of the person. People who have mostly positive emotions (such as being happy and jovial most of the time) have their ulcers heal faster than people who exhibit negative emotions (such as bitterness and anger). For the former category of people, their bodies seem to be fighting them by releasing harmful chemicals into the stomach, resulting in the stomach walls being eroded by the acidic chemicals released as a result of unhappiness. Therefore, people who are always unhappy or whose hearts are hardly merry are prone to suffering from many kinds of ill health. By forgiving, much of these effects could be prevented or substantially minimized.

## Forgiving Removes the Offender's Accountability

Another common misconception about forgiveness is that it allows the offender to get away with an offense without being held accountable for it. If not, it is thought or assumed that forgiving another person excuses the person from the crime committed or hurt caused. Finally, it is often believed the forgiving is akin to—or means—having the offended person completely over with whatever the offender did or caused. These three related issues have, from time to time, stood in the way of forgiveness because many people are not ready to do them. Since they are not yet prepared to do them—or cannot do them in the first place—they do not forgive. The result is that they hold on to negative emotions, bitter thoughts, rage, and even vengeance toward the offender for a long time.

It so happens that some of the offended people may genuinely want to let go of the negative thoughts of resentment, bitterness, and vengeance. However, they cannot do it because of their false or misplaced understanding of what it means to forgive. If not, they are concerned that the person will never be punished for the offense committed, will be excluded from the crime, or are over and done with the harm caused by the offender. The truth is that forgiveness does not—and needs not—have anything to do with any of these issues. First, it is a reality that forgiving has nothing to do with excusing a person for the person's offense. Instead, the two are quite different issues that have to be approached differently and with different outcomes. The offended person cannot usually excuse the offender of the offense. Even if, somehow, the angry person did something that resulted in the offense being committed, it does not change the fact that the offender did something that hurt or caused harm to the offended person.

As long as someone got hurt or emotionally injured as a result of another person's actions or inactions, the latter person is liable for the offense. In essence, the level of liability of the offended person in the offense is not a consideration when it comes to forgiving. There are no factors to consider when forgiving except that it is a command from God and there is a need to release the other person from any claims to be compensated for the loss or hurt suffered.[14] In any situation where there has been an offense, admission of that offense is usually a vital starting point in the process of forgiveness. The disclosure that the offense was not just real but also hurting and inexcusable shows that a person may be ready to forgive just as God pardoned the person when he or she offended God.

Perhaps the right way to look at this specific misconception is to consider God as the offended person. When a person offends God, and God forgives the person as is God's nature, forgiveness does not mean that the offense has been justified or that the person can no longer be held to account for the action. At the end of it all, every human being will stand at the judgment seat of God to be judged for their actions and inactions in the world.

Writing to the Church at Corinth, Paul made this clear to them:

> For we must all appear before the judgment seat of Christ;
> that every one may receive the things done in his body,
> according to that he hath done, whether it be good or
> bad.[15]

Debates about God's judgment are beyond the scope of this book. However, the reality is that there is a judgment to come for every person. The same God who forgives sin will be judging all people for their worldly sins.

Yet this ought not to mean that it is in vain to forgive because ultimately, everyone will deal with the consequences of their sins. This is why forgiveness of sins is something that mostly serves an earthly purpose. Rather than remain on the offender's emotional hook or prison, one can forgive and be set free from the hook. In the same way, God chose to forgive humanity because he had a plan for humanity's sins. All that keeping track of sin and having to remember what everyone did was not God's idea of a relationship with his creation. Through Jesus Christ, God no longer chose to remember sins once they have been forgiven. Still, God does not usually let people get away with the consequences of their

---

[14] Larry D. Ellis, *Forgiveness: Unleashing a Transformational Process* (Denver, CO: Adoration Publishing Company, 2010), 21.
[15] 2 Corinthians 5:10 KJV.

sins against God and other people. First, sinning against other people is sinning against God. Therefore, people ought not to sin and assume that as long as they have not sinned against God, then they need not forgive or be forgiven. Once sin is committed, God will deal with its consequences at the appropriate time. This is the common practice not just in the Old Testament but also in the New Testament.

When Adam sinned against God in the Garden of Eden, he still had to deal with the consequences of his sins, whereby God banished him and his wife Eve from the Garden of Eden.[16] When Cain killed his brother, Abel, out of jealousy, Cain was made to pay for his sins by being banished from the family and being made to wander the face of the earth. When Moses angrily struck the rock in the desert instead of talking to it to release the word as commanded by God, he met the ultimate punishment of death in the desert before entering the Promised Land. It is written that:

> Then Moses raised his arm and struck the rock twice with his staff. Water gushed out, and the community and their livestock drank. But the Lord said to Moses and Aaron, "Because you did not trust in me enough to honor me as holy in the sight of the Israelites, you will not bring this community into the land I give them."[17]

When Jacob deceived his brother, Esau, out of his birthright, God allowed him to be driven out of his father's house. He had to seek refuge in the land of his uncle, Laban.[18] When Jonah defied God's order to preach the gospel of forgiveness to the Nineveh and instead went to Tarshish, he was punished when he had to be swallowed by a big fish and was later forced to go to Nineveh or risk death.[19] As these examples show, God forgave the people who sinned against him and other people, but they were still accountable for their actions and had to bear the consequences of those actions. Therefore, forgiving does not excuse a person of their offense.

---

[16] Genesis 3:23 NIV.
[17] Numbers 20:11–13 NIV.
[18] Genesis 28:1–19 KJV.
[19] Jonah 1:1–17 NIV.

The reality is that every person is ultimately held accountable for their actions. However, it is the responsibility of God and not human beings to hold people responsible for their actions or inactions. When it comes to the issue of sin, in particular, God expressly states that he must repay people of their wrongdoing both against God and against humanity:

> Dearly beloved, avenge not yourselves, but rather give place unto wrath: for it is written, Vengeance *is* mine; I will repay.[20]

> To me belongeth vengeance and recompense; their foot shall slide in due time: for the day of their calamity is at hand, and the things that shall come upon them make haste.[21]

It is also important to note that forgiving a person does not, in any way, mean that whatever the person did was right or justified. If anything, the very fact that a person's actions or inactions hurt another person means that those actions or inactions were wrong or unnecessary. Alternatively, these actions may have been done at the wrong time or were targeted at the wrong person.

Moreover, it never really matters what the offended person did—or did not do—that warranted or led to the offense. All offenses must result from something the offended person did or did not do. Even if the offended person had a role to play in the offense and feels that the offense may have been justified somehow, there has to be forgiving. In the same way, the offender has to be forgiven regardless of whether or not it was their fault that the offense was committed.

The most crucial issue is that forgiving a person has nothing to do with the liability of the person for the offense or the offender not being held accountable for the offense. Instead, forgiveness is independent of the nature and magnitude of the offense. It is not uncommon for people to refuse to forgive because they think the crime committed is too big to be

---

[20] Romans 12:19 KJV.
[21] Deuteronomy 32:35 KJV.

overlooked or the reason that the offender acted irresponsibly and willfully. Under such circumstances, it seems not just okay but also justifiable to not forgive. However, this could not be further from the truth.

The reality is that forgiveness is not dependent on the nature of the offense committed or its magnitude. It is also independent of the attitude of the offender. For both "big" and "small" offenses, there has to be forgiveness. If anything, there is no such thing as a big or small offense or sin before God. Instead, all wrongdoing is considered sinful and must be atoned.

In the same way, all offenses are equal in the sight of God and must be similar in the view of humanity. Therefore, the magnitude of the offense should never matter. The only issue that ought to matter is the existence of an offense. As long as an offense has been committed, forgiveness ought to follow. In the same way, forgiveness has to be offered regardless of the offender's attitude. It so happens that people who commit offenses are usually proud and disrespectful. They hardly ever care about anything or anyone else but themselves. They are often haughty, and their pride cannot allow them to be apologetic or repentant of their actions. However, it is also possible for offenders to be seemingly polite and caring people whose actions and behaviors might indicate that the offense was not intentional.

Still, both categories of offenders need to be forgiven because forgiveness has to be offered without regard to the attitude and behavior of the offender.[22] At the right time, God can be expected to deal with the offender if, indeed, God deems it right to do so. This is also an essential issue because sometimes people forgive but then keep asking or praying to God to punish the offender for the offense. This may be a natural approach to a problem by humans, but it is not the attitude God expects of his people. Because vengeance belongs to God, he does not expect human beings to make decisions for him on how and when to avenge or punish someone. Such an attitude may cause God not to punish the person. Instead, God expects offended people to pray for those who have offended them instead of scolding them or wishing them evil. When offended or hurt people pray for their offenders, God's wrath gets kindled against the offender. On the contrary, God's anger tends to relent when offended people attempt to use

---

[22] Larry D. Ellis, *Forgiveness: Unleashing a Transformational Process* (Denver, CO: Adoration Publishing Company, 2010), 31.

their power to get revenge. That is how God works, and his working is in stark contrast to the operations of humankind.

Therefore, when an offender is truly and genuinely forgiven by the offended party, this opens up the door for God to deal with the person as God sees it best. If anything, one of the purposes of forgiving is being able to surrender the hurt and harm to God, who is the fair judge. Forgiving is akin to the offended person acknowledging they are surrendering everything to God and trusting in God's wisdom to deal with the situation as God sees best. It is surrendering one's will to God's will. When one surrenders their will and allows God's will to be done, it does not mean that God is under any obligation to act—let alone work in the ways desired or preferred by the offended person. Instead, surrendering to one's will to God's will means trusting God to do the absolute best under the circumstances and according to his purposes. This may include punishing the offender or letting him go scot-free. Painful and difficult as this may be, it is how God intended forgiveness to be.

God himself makes it clear that offenses ought not to be condoned by condemning those who argue that wrong actions are acceptable or harmless:

> Woe unto them that call evil good, and good evil; that put
> darkness for light, and light for darkness; that put bitter
> for sweet, and sweet for bitter![23]

In the same way, God is opposed to the idea of offended people pretending that the offense never took place or occurred. One of the best examples of God forgiving sin but holding a person to account for the person's sin is King David. When David took Uriah's wife after killing her husband (by placing him in the battle frontlines), God was not pleased. After David begged for mercy and was forgiven of the sin, the consequence was that the son born to David as a result of the sin died. This was even though David did all that was humanly possible to have the child live.

---

[23] Isaiah 5:20 KJV.

Moreover, David's sin was recorded so that generations of Israelites would be able to remember them and fear God.[24]

David did not pretend that no sin had taken place and readily admitted his wrongdoing. God did not act as though there had been no sin even though David was the king of Israel. If anything, the fact that David was the king made God want the sin to be known to the entire world to serve as a lesson to other people. This does not mean that unless offenders repent of their sins like David, they are not to be forgiven. David did well to repent because this sin was a sin against God and not humanity:

> Against you, you only, have I sinned and done what is evil in your sight, so you are right in your verdict and justified when you judge.[25]

Still, God may have forgiven anyway. Therefore, forgiveness does not mean that the offender is excused of their offense or that they can get away with the offense without punishment. The two are mutually exclusive and independent of each other.

By extension, agreeing to forgive does not mean that other people can take advantage of the offended person. This is one of the main reasons people tend to be extremely reluctant to forgive. These people reason that if they forgive, the offender—and others who know about the offense—may perceive the offended person as weak or incapable of doing anything about the offense. Therefore, they may become inclined to taking advantage of the offended person. Many people want to take advantage of others for their gain.[26] This has happened mostly in situations concerning financial transactions or disputes concerning money. Most of the time, the offended person feels that he or she has been duped and taken advantage of by the other—and that forgiving is not an option.

A typical example is where a brother in trouble of being evicted from his house borrows money from a fellow brother to pay the house rent in arrears. The money is supposed to be paid back after some time, but the

---

[24] 2 Samuel 12:9–13 NIV.

[25] Psalm 51:4 NIV.

[26] Anthony Bash, *Forgiveness: A Theology*, vol. 19, Cascade Companions (Eugene, OR: Cascade Books, 2015), 34.

deadline comes and goes without any word from the borrower. This is even though the borrower's financial situation has dramatically improved. They are financially well off enough to repay the owed debt, but they choose not to pay. Under such circumstances, the lender has several options at his disposal; the top of which is to decide to forgive and move on. However, the owed brother can also choose to harbor resentment against the borrower and keep rehashing the matter with him. Finally, the lender could make the decision that he will not lend money to the brother again—or any other person for that matter.

In this situation, the decision on whether or not to forgive is not dependent on the debt being repaid. If anything, the lender could still refuse to lend the money to the brother even if the payment is refunded.

A person can choose to forgive and then deal with the actual or likely effects or consequences of the offense later on. Forgiving and not lending the person money in the future is an example of the lender protecting oneself from having to be taken advantage of by the borrower. There is no requirement for the lender to lend money to the brother ever again or even to any other person. However, there is a requirement for them to forgive. Indeed, people who have been forgiven of their debts or who offenses have been forgiven tend to be increasingly inclined to re-offend or take advantage of the situation. Those who could not repay financial debts will attempt to borrow again. Those who stole from a person may want to steal again. Those who committed infidelity may be tempted to do it again. Does this mean that the offended person who forgave the first time is being taken advantage of by the offender? Well, it all depends on how the person views and understands forgiveness.

A true conception of forgiveness should enable the person to understand that they are being taken advantage of in some way. After all, any repeat offense is an indication of the fact that the offender took—or is taking—advantage of the offended person (at least from human beings). Still, it should have nothing to do with forgiveness. As long as an offense has been committed, there has to be forgiveness. Afterward, the person could choose how to respond to avoid being taken advantage of in the future. It is also true that human nature is sinful, and human beings can't avoid offending. They have been doing this since Adam's fall in the Garden of Eden and will probably continue sinning till the Day of Judgment. Therefore, a person ought not to always think that when offended, the offender is taking advantage of them. On the contrary, it is possible that the offender is just trapped into a cycle of sinning and would wish not to sin again:

> The wicked borrow and do not repay, but the righteous give generously.[27]

This verse contrasts the behaviors of two types of people: the wicked and the righteous. The former do not repay when they borrow, but the latter are not prevented from giving freely as a result of their loans not being reciprocated. This seems to be the central message in this verse (even though other people may interpret it differently). The psalmist must have had in mind a situation where someone or some people had borrowed money from others and refused to pay, perhaps expecting that the lender would cease lending. However, the lenders kept lending even as their money was not getting repaid. This is the attitude that people need to forgive. They have to come to the point where they realize that their giving is independent of the status of the loan.[28] They keep giving whether or not the loan has been repaid or not been repaid. Because forgiveness is a form of giving where the offended person gives up any claim to be compensated for the loss or hurt suffered, it also needs to be "given" or done regardless of whether or not the debt is repaid.

Many people regret at least some of their offenses and even wonder how they happened. Many are the times when offenses occur because of the human tendency to offend. As a result, human beings must also be ready to be hurt just as they keep offending. Every individual has the discretion to ensure other people do not take advantage of them by acting prudently:

> The simple believe anything, but the prudent give thought to their steps.[29]

---

[27] Psalm 37:21 NIV.

[28] Anthony Bash, *Forgiveness: A Theology*, vol. 19, Cascade Companions (Eugene, OR: Cascade Books, 2015), 44.

[29] Proverbs 14:15 NIV.

The apostle Paul also exhorted the Church at Galatia to "not be deceived: God cannot be mocked. A man reaps what he sows."[30] It is best not to believe everything to gauge every issue based on its merit. Yet all these have nothing to do with forgiveness. Put differently: an indiscretion cannot justify the refusal to forgive.

## Forgiveness Means Reestablishing the Past Relationships

Just like forgiving does not mean excusing the offender or letting them go scot-free, forgiving does not mean reestablishing relationships with the offender.[31] This is a misconception that has prevented forgiveness from taking place on many occasions and in many instances. The issue of relationships here is essential because for an offense to occur, the offender and the offended people must have been in the form of a link that brought them together. If anything, people who are not in contact with each other or who have no kind of association or affiliation cannot practically hurt each other. Even if the two people live apart from each other or are physically and geographically separated by a considerable distance, they can still hurt each other as long as there is communication (or any other form of contact) between them. Therefore, it is quite commonplace for people to falsely assume or expect that forgiving the person who offended them would entail or include reestablishing the relationship they had before the offense.

The reality is that it is upon the offended person to decide on how to approach the relationship. On the one hand, he or she may choose to have the connection reestablished—and if so, at what time and based on which specific conditions (if any at all). On the other hand, he or she may decide not to reestablish the relationship or to reestablish it after a long time—perhaps after the offender makes amends or restitution to the offended person. Regardless of which choice is made, these considerations ought not to influence the decision on forgiving. In essence, the offended person is duty bound to forgive regardless of whether he or she wants the relationship reestablished. Moreover, forgiving has nothing to do with the

---

[30] Galatians 6:7 NIV.

[31] Derek Prince, *The Three Most Powerful Words: Discovering the Freedom of Releasing the Ones Who Hurt Us* (Charlotte, NC: Derek Prince Ministries, 2006), 39.

direction the previous connection will take. Instead, it has everything to do with the present problems, which are usually that offenders feel like they have specific claims to be compensated for the loss or hurt suffered. People are free to become friends again or to continue their past business or other relationship. However, this is dependent on the choices they make themselves and has nothing to do with forgiveness.

In the same way, it is possible for people to reestablish their relationships but truly forgive each other. This shows that relationships between people do not—or ought not to—determine whether or not there is forgiveness. If forgiveness were based on the ability of the two people to reestablish friendships or relationships, then forgiveness would have become more complicated. This is because one of the reasons people are fearful or concerned about forgiving is that they do not want to be hurt again, especially by the same person. The risk of not just getting hurt again but the chances of being hurt by the same person significantly increase when the former relationship is reestablished. This happens because the two people have to stay connected again—the situation that makes it possible for one to hurt the other. As was noted before, it is not practically possible for a person to be injured by another if the two have no form of contact or between them, be it physical or not.

Breaking up and letting go of the past relationship may help the offended person forgive more quickly because it minimizes the risk of being offended again. This ought not to mean that if the connection is severed, there is a guarantee that no offense will be committed again. On the contrary, people who have moved on and even gone their separate ways have still found ways to hurt each other, especially if there is some form of connection between them. For instance, mutual friends get retained when two people offend each other and cannot reestablish their former relationship. These mutual friends can—and often do—convey messages between the two people, and these messages can cause more annoyance or hurt for the offended person. This is the basis for arguing that the risk of reoffending greatly diminishes when contact between the offender and the offended person is limited or eliminated.

The truth is that forgiveness does not even require the two people to meet for it to take place. Instead, it occurs in the offended person's heart when that person makes the deliberate choice to release the offender from the expectation mentioned above that he or she will make right whatever hurt he or she caused as well as stop associating the offender with the offense. These two actions do not require the two people concerned to be present together as they all depend on the offended person. It is the offended person who has to decide how to respond to the offense and its resultant effects on the person. This explains why offenders hardly ever play a role in the process of forgiveness because they are scarcely present when it happens. If offenders can be available, then it is okay since it can allow the two people to start afresh. If the offender goes ahead and apologizes for the offense, it is better for the relationship between the two and for forgiveness to happen.

However, the presence of the offender—as well as whatever they do as a result of their presence—ought not to be the determinant of whether or not forgiveness takes or—even worse—how it takes place. If this were to be the case, then forgiveness would not take place as it should, or it would be thought that forgiveness happened when in truth it did not. This is because it is not possible to ascertain human motivations in the actions they take or even the words they speak. A person may seek to be forgiven but not out of a genuine desire for forgiveness but with another motivation, such as taking advantage of the offended person. Another may be present in a reconciliation meeting but not truly facilitate the reconciliation process to try to determine what the offended person is doing about the offense. This is a reality about human nature that cannot be wished away. This is why there are times when individual critical decisions affecting a person are best taken in solitude as opposed to in the presence of many people, and forgiving is one of them. Since second or even third parties add little, if any, value to the process, they may as well be left out.

In this specific regard, forgiveness ought to be approached similarly as prayer, where it is better to pray in secrecy than in public. When Jesus wanted to make some of his most intense prayers to God, he often did so out of earshot of even his most trusted disciples (John, Peter, and Andrew). This happened, for instance, in the Garden of Gethsemane just before Jesus was crucified as well as when Jesus went to raise Lazarus from the dead. These two incidents (among others) indicate that prayer is most effective when one prays alone (unless the prayers specifically and purposely need to be made within a group setting). In the same way, the presence of other people tends to hinder rather than facilitate forgiveness. That is why forgiveness does not require the offender and offended person to meet or agree. Had this been the case, it would be impossible for dead people to be forgiven since the living and the dead cannot meet up. This, in turn, explains why living people have been able to forgive people who have died—it is because forgiveness takes place in the heart of the offended person and not in the meeting place between the offender and the offended person.

There is no doubt that forgiving can have the intended or unintended effect of helping two people reestablish a past relationship. This happens when the offended person can get the peace of mind necessary to free them from debilitating feelings of anger. Anger is such an intense emotion that it can practically result in physical disability when the offended person becomes powerless to act. This occurs when the person's feelings are so strong and intense that they cloud and impede normal thinking processes. A person acts rationally only to the extent that they have the opportunity to think clearly without any impediments. When a person forgives, one of the outcomes is that the person is empowered to recognize and appreciate the pain suffered as a result of the offense without allowing the pain to be the defining factor. Because the offended person can only think clearly and rationally after letting go of the deeply held feelings of anger, rage, and resentment, forgiveness allows them to appraise the situation more objectively and understand the need and importance of moving on. This, in turn, facilitates reconciliation.

Forgiveness can also help the offender become more inclined toward the reestablishment of the past relationship because it eliminates feelings of mutual distrust.[32] When two people cannot trust each other, they can't be friends or have a different type of relationship. The suspicion keeps them apart regardless of how much they try to get together. Forgiveness eliminates distrust to a significant degree and therefore paves the way for reconciliation.[33] Once two people are reconciled, they are more likely to reestablish their past relationship. Thus, forgiving may facilitate the

---

[32] Robert Jeffress, *When Forgiveness Doesn't Make Sense* (Colorado Springs, CO: WaterBrook, 2000), 12.
[33] Fraser Watts and Liz Gulliford, *Forgiveness in Context: Theology and Psychology in Creative Dialogue* (London, New York: T&T Clark, 2004), 20.

process of repairing broken links, but it needs not be dependent on the repair of such relations. In the same manner, the offender remains legally accountable regardless of whether or not forgiveness has taken place.

As discussed in other sections of this chapter, the mere fact that a person forgives another does not remove or eliminate the offender's liability before the law or before other people (society). Some offended people attempt to get forgiveness from the offended person as a way of escaping other issues they are liable for without addressing them. For instance, the offender may try to seek forgiveness in the belief that it will help them reestablish a friendship and prevent the offended person from taking further action. This is a misconception since a person can forgive another but still seek legal redress if this is applicable. While reestablishment of past relationships is likely to prevent the offended person from pursuing any other remedies from the offender, it is not usually a guarantee that this will happen.

History is full of examples of people who forgave those who hurt them and even reestablished relations with them but still took some form of action against the offender. The story of David and God exemplifies this. When David sinned against God by taking the wife of Uriah and killing her husband, God punished David even after David was forgiven of the sin. When the sin was forgiven, God still referred to David as "a man after my own heart." This was when he said to Saul through Samuel:

> But now your kingdom will not endure; the Lord has sought out a man after his own heart and appointed him ruler of his people because you have not kept the Lord's command.[34]

Among other possible interpretations, this verse indicates that God was able to reestablish his previous relationship with David. However, the act of forgiving was independent of the reestablishment of the relationship. Even after the connection had been reestablished, God still ensured that David experienced the consequences of his actions. At one time, David's son rose against him and slept with David's wives:

---

[34] 2 Samuel 13:14 NIV.

And Ahithophel said unto Absalom, "Go in unto thy father's concubines, which he hath left to keep the house; and all Israel shall hear that thou art abhorred of thy father: then shall the hands of all that are with thee be strong." So they spread Absalom a tent upon the top of the house; Absalom went in unto his father's concubines in the sight of all Israel.[35]

This was one of the greatest humiliations David had to endure in his life. Yet this happened as part of God's way of holding David accountable for the act of killing Uriah and taking his wife as his own.

## Forgiving Should Come Only When the Offense No Longer Hurts

The other common misconception about forgiveness is the tendency to think that forgiveness can only happen when the offense is not hurting any longer. This misconception is based on the false view that as long as one continues hurting or the effect of the offense remains, it is justifiable not to forgive. This could not be further from the truth. The reality is that an offense might not stop hurting until there is forgiveness. This means that instead of waiting for the offense to stop hurting before one can forgive, people ought to do the exact opposite: they need to forgive first, and the offense will stop hurting. Yet there is a caution: this applies only to the emotional hurt caused by an offense. Other forms of hurting, such as a physical injury or stolen money, may not necessarily cease hurting as a result of forgiveness. However, as a person gets over the negative emotions associated with not forgiving, they become more likely to experience emotional healing and other forms of release.

Jesus was hurt both emotionally and physically beyond what any human being could endure, yet he did not wait to forgive until he had healed from the hurt or until he was no longer hurting. Instead, he forgave almost as soon as his torturers and killers had finished their work. They were not yet done with him by the time he cried to God, asking that God

---

[35] 2 Samuel 16:21–23 KJV.

forgives them. This represents the right attitude toward forgiving—it never has to wait until the offense no longer hurts. Instead, it has to be done as soon as possible to free the offended person from the emotional pain and hurt that results from losses or hurts suffered. Many times, the offense will never stop hurting. Some offenses are so grave that, regardless of what the person does, the resultant hurting or harm cannot go away.

A good example would be concerning the offense of first-degree murder when someone kills another person even though they are innocent and have done nothing wrong. Perhaps their only crime is belonging to a particular race or ethnicity, which happened during the Holocaust. Back then, Nazi Germany's goal in exterminating the Jews was based on pure evil and the distorted view that Jews were troublemakers who did not deserve to live. As a result, millions were herded like cattle into concentration camps in Germany and throughout territories occupied and controlled by the Nazis. Millions lost their lives in this manner.

For the children, friends, brothers, parents, and sisters of those who were mercilessly executed in this manner, forgiving can be challenging, especially considering that the hurt occasioned by the offense remains. Honestly, one cannot forget the pain of losing a loved one. Even if the pain somehow eases, it almost always comes back whenever those left behind have to think of or recall what happened. In such circumstances, one cannot possibly expect to wait for the hurt or pain of the offense to end before forgiving because the offense may never truly cease hurting.

## Forgiveness Must Be Preceded by an Apology

Another common and significant misconception about forgiveness is that if it has to be granted to anyone, then it must be preceded by an apology from the offender. By far, this misconception has been responsible for arguably the most instances when forgiveness has been withheld or denied. Among both Christians and non-Christians, it is not uncommon for one to cite the lack of an apology from the offender as the reason for not forgiving the person.[36] According to this misconception, an apology, regardless of whether it is formally or informally given, shows that the

---

[36] Fraser Watts and Liz Gulliford, *Forgiveness in Context: Theology and Psychology in Creative Dialogue* (London, New York: T&T Clark, 2004), 29.

offender is genuinely apologetic or remorseful and feels sorry for the offense committed. It supposedly shows that the offender did not commit the offense intentionally and that he or she regrets whatever happened.

The reality is that basing forgiveness on the ability of the offender to apologize for the offense is deceptive and misleading. Offenders rarely apologize for their offenses. As was noted before, many offenders lack even the slightest idea that they have offended someone (let alone the need for them to apologize to the person hurt). In this regard, the offended person may wait an eternity for an apology to come—and it might never come. Even if the offender is well aware of the offense committed, it is only in rare circumstances that an apology would go forth. If it does come, it could be forced and not genuine, which happens when people are forced to ask for forgiveness. For instance, it is not uncommon for Christians to compel fellow believers to apologize for offenses or forgive each other. Similarly, even nonbelievers sometimes force offending people to apologize for some additional benefit to be obtained from the offended person.

Just because an offender offers an apology does not mean—or ought not to say— they are genuinely apologetic. Different reasons could motivate an offender to apologize, and some of these reasons have nothing to do with feelings of genuine remorse or regret over the offense committed. On many occasions, the people apologizing do so because they need something from the offended—something that cannot be obtained without the two people first making up after a past offense. For instance, many apologies are offered to preserve a friendship (or reestablish it) or for a benefactor to continue aiding. This does not mean that there are no genuine apologies.

On the contrary, some offending people genuinely feel the need to apologize for offenses committed and are truly and genuinely sincere and remorseful about their offenses. For such ones, the offense is usually a mistake or an oversight on their part. They take personal responsibility for the offense and want to be forgiven. Unfortunately, such people tend to form a small minority consisting of a few people who understand that forgiveness helps the offended person more than the offender.

Still, the most crucial consideration when it comes to the issue of forgiving is that it needs to be done regardless of whether or not there is an apology. Other than the fact that most people will not ask to be forgiven even when they are fully aware that they offended another person, many people die with many committed and unresolved offenses. Therefore, it is practically impossible for dead people to offer an apology to the living for the living to forgive. In essence, it is hypocritical for anyone to require an apology before forgiving because an apology cannot come from the dead. Since many people have died having offended others and never having sought to be forgiven (or having offered an apology), there is no way the people they hurt will ever get an apology from them.

This implies that requiring or demanding an apology before forgiving an offender is a selfish approach to forgiving because it effectively means that such people cannot forgive those who died. This is an important issue when one considers the fact that the death of an individual who offended a living person does not necessarily bring an end to the emotional suffering on the part of the offended person. Instead, some offenses keep hurting (or even become more hurtful) even upon the death of the offender. Since the dead person can't ask to be forgiven, it is only prudent that the offended person forgives and moves on if healing has to take place:

> If we confess our sins, he is faithful and just and will forgive us our sins and purify us from all unrighteousness[37]

> Do not judge, and you will not be judged. Do not condemn, and you will not be condemned. Forgive, and you will be forgiven."[38]

Refusing to forgive because the offended person is waiting for the offender to ask for forgiveness is a big gamble if the offender is still alive since there are no guarantees that such an apology will be sought. However, refusing to forgive a dead person is tantamount to insanity since the dead will never rise to offer apologies.

It is also important to note that the ultimate goal of forgiving on the part of the offended person is for true healing to be achieved. Forgiving is supposed to help the offended person overcome the hurting caused by the offense. Since every offense—especially if it is committed by close

---

[37] 1 John 1:9 NIV.
[38] Luke 6:37 NIV.

friend or ally—hurts, healing from the hurt emotionally, mentally, and sometimes even physically is paramount. The problem with waiting for an apology before forgiving is that even in the highly unlikely event that an apology is offered, it will not take away the hurt or undo the harm caused. In essence, it is not an apology that takes away the pain or damage caused by an offense. Instead, such hurting or injury can only be taken away by forgiving because forgiving others attracts God's forgiveness.[39]

> If you forgive other people when they sin against you, your heavenly Father will also forgive you. But if you do not forgive others their sins, your Father will not forgive your sins.[40]

The fact that every offended person needs to heal from the hurt (or harm) with or without an apology underscores the need for forgiveness not to be tied to an apology. Even if the offended person needed an apology, it would better if a pardon was granted first—after which, the offended person would wait for an apology. This would help the offended person a lot more than waiting for an apology before forgiving (or before deciding whether to forgive).

It is also worth adding that some apologies are never followed by forgiving. Human nature is sometimes such that holding onto past offenses helps sustain other aspects of life. This could explain why many offended people have refused to forgive their offenders even after the latter have apologized. This shows that for some people, refusing to forgive others gives them a sense of authority or control over their offenders. They seem to enjoy being able to control and manipulate their offenders for their selfish ends. Therefore, tying forgiveness to an apology is an inherently flawed way of looking at forgiveness. The two ought not to be tied together.

This line of reasoning is not meant to minimize or underrate the value of an apology. The reality is that apologies do work wonders when it comes to the area of forgiveness because they often pave the way for forgiveness to take place. This even occurs among people and regarding issues where it

---

[39] Robert Jeffress, *When Forgiveness Doesn't Make Sense* (Colorado Springs, CO: WaterBrook, 2000), 22.
[40] Matthew 6:14–15 NIV.

seemed that amnesty would not come. An apology seems to have the effect of breaking down many barriers that can hinder forgiveness. For instance, an apology softens the offended person and makes them realize that the offender may not have intended for the offense to occur in the first place.

Many are the times and instances when it is only through an apology that the offended person gets to talk with the offender about the offense. This provides an opportunity for both parties to review what happened and understand each other's role in the offense.[41] This way, the resultant mutual understanding of the events that led to the offense can significantly soften the offended person to the point of forgiving without any conditions. In most cases where people refuse to forgive, the underlying reason is that they think the offender committed the offense on purpose and to harm the offended person. When the two discuss what happened—as happens when an apology is offered—forgiving tends to follow almost naturally. Still, an apology should never be a precondition for forgiveness since the former is seldom forthcoming.

Forgiveness needs not to be preceded by an apology, but it is worth adding that the Bible also seems to suggest that forgiveness ought to be based on an apology from the offender. This view is mainly associated with Jesus's teachings as recorded by Luke. This does not mean that the Bible is contradictory or that Jesus's teachings on forgiveness contradict those by his disciples. On the contrary, these could mostly be the result of differences in how the teachings of Jesus on the subject matter were recorded and interpreted by the writers of the four Gospels. Just as with several other instructions on different issues, the Synoptic Gospels (Matthew, Mark, and Luke) seem to be slightly different from that of John. Usually, there are slight variations in interpretation between the various authors, but the differences are mainly a result of the issues they wanted to emphasize rather than differences in reality. Even the Synoptic Gospels may have slight variations among them based on the fact that the different authors wanted their audiences to understand specific issues the most and, as such, put more emphasis on those aspects.

It is against this backdrop that Luke's account of forgiveness seems to

<hr>

[41] Fraser Watts and Liz Gulliford, *Forgiveness in Context: Theology and Psychology in Creative Dialogue* (London, New York: T&T Clark, 2004), 26.

be slightly different from the accounts of the other Gospels. Unlike the other Gospels, the Gospel of Luke appears to require that offended persons apologize for their offenses if they need to be forgiven:

> If your brother sins, rebuke him, and if he repents, forgive him. If he sins against you seven times in a day, and seven times comes back to you and says, "I repent," forgive him.[42]

This verse uses the conditional word "if" at least three times. This, in itself, suggests that forgiving is conditional. It is based on the offender's repenting. However, it also makes it clear that forgiveness ought not to be withheld regardless of the number of times the offender requires it.

It appears that Luke intended to emphasize the aspect that offenders or sinners will need to be forgiven and that offended people need not withhold it from them. This is regardless of the number of times the person needs forgiveness. Moreover, repentance may not necessarily mean the same thing as seeking an apology. It depends on the exact context in which it is being used. Some people who claim to be repenting are hardly ever apologetic. Instead, they do it out of malice or intending to achieve some other selfish end. It may be argued that perhaps Jesus intended to distinguish between repeated offenses and offenses that were committed only once or less frequently. In scripture, as mentioned earlier, the focus is on the offender who sins seven times. This is a large number of offenses for a single day. It would be absurd for anyone to expect to be forgiven for seven offenses all committed within the same day unless they apologize first.

In this regard, repentance or apology is used to indicate the offender did not commit the offense on purpose. Otherwise, such offenses would suggest that the offender was doing them purposely and intending to cause harm to or hurt the offended person deliberately. Even God himself is usually not willing to forgive people who sin with arrogance and show no remorse or are unwilling to repent. That is why he cautions that those who

---

[42] Luke 17:3–4 NIV.

go on sinning after they have received forgiveness may never be forgiven again but would be condemned to death:

> If we sin willfully after that we have received the knowledge of the truth, there remaineth no more sacrifice for sins, But a certain fearful looking for of judgment and fiery indignation, which shall devour the adversaries. He that despised Moses's law died without mercy under two or three witnesses: Of how much sorer punishment, suppose ye, shall he be thought worthy, who hath trodden under foot the Son of God, and hath counted the blood of the covenant, wherewith he was sanctified, an unholy thing, and hath done despite unto the Spirit of grace?[43]

The bottom line is that forgiveness is demanded of everyone, especially believers, at all times.[44] However, God also expects—but not necessarily requires—that offenders exhibit an attitude of repentance to be forgiven. Even if they do not practically come to the offended person and ask to be forgiven, they can exhibit an attitude of repentance by not repeating the offense over and over again. If offenders repeat their offenses, it shows that they are unrepentant—and God might not necessarily forgive them. After all, the ultimate forgiveness is by God.

---

[43] Hebrews 10:26–29 KJV.

[44] Everett L. Worthington Jr., *Handbook of Forgiveness* (Abingdon, United Kingdom: Routledge, 2007), 20.

# CHAPTER 2

# WHAT IS FORGIVENESS?

One of the hardest questions that people can be asked is whether they have forgiven their offenders. Most of the time, the response is usually in the affirmative. In reality, though, forgiveness has not taken place at all—and if it has, then it may not be genuine or from deep down in one's heart. It is also possible that the person who claims to have forgiven means it but has no idea what true forgiveness is or entails. This makes it essential to understand the meaning of forgiveness. Unfortunately, what some people consider to be forgiveness does not constitute forgiveness. This is one of the reasons why there are so many misconceptions about forgiveness. Many people have different views about forgiveness (and what it either entails or does not entail). Similarly, different viewpoints exist when it comes to the meaning of forgiveness.

For one to understand what forgiveness is, there has to be an understanding of the different feelings and emotions that are associated with being hurt or offended by another person. This is because these emotions and feelings have such a significant impact on the offended person that one would immediately know if forgiveness has taken place by determining whether the negative feelings and emotions associated with being hurt still exist or have disappeared. Put differently, one of the most effective ways of knowing if forgiveness has taken place is by ascertaining whether or not—and the extent to which—negative feelings and emotions occasioned or triggered by an offense still manifest or have disappeared. If they have gone, there is a high possibility that forgiveness has taken place.

If, on the other hand, these negative feelings and emotions persist and are felt strongly, forgiveness has not taken place.

When another person has hurt someone, one of the most common and enduring manifestations of the offense is the tendency by the offended person to stew and complain about the offense or the incident from time to time. Most offended people look forward to an opportunity to talk about the offense, and when this opportunity does not come, they may keep replaying the issue in their minds.[45] This seems to be a critical coping mechanism for offended people. Sometimes offended people can try hard and be able to live without having to think about the offender and the hurtful offense committed. However, this hardly lasts long enough. Instead, the hurt person will soon come to think of the offense after some time.

This means that there may be variations in the length of time from one person to another, but all offended people find themselves thinking and rethinking the hurtful events and offenses from time to time, especially when they are made to remember or think about the actual events that took place. This almost always occurs when the offended person meets or sees the offender, at which point the memories come flooding back to one's mind. Even when the offended person has almost healed from the hurt or has managed to conceal the damage from other people carefully, the pain is immediately latched onto at the presence, mention, or thought of the offender.

Therefore, one of the surest ways of ascertaining whether or not real and genuine forgiveness has taken place is to carefully examine the offended person's behaviors and emotions when in the presence of the offender or when the discussion centers on the offender. As long as there are negative emotions, forgiveness has not taken place. Similarly, forgiveness has not taken place if the offended person's behavior is indifferent or defiant. The offended person is usually wondering why they had to be hurt so badly and the wrong that was done to justify or warrant such deep hurt. There are also thoughts of how the situation could have been avoided in the first place.

---

[45] Fraser Watts and Liz Gulliford, *Forgiveness in Context: Theology and Psychology in Creative Dialogue* (London, New York: T&T Clark, 2004), 20.

Moreover, the offended person will often think about how he or she could have avoided the situation that ultimately resulted in the offense and the associated hurt. When considered together, these thoughts, feelings, and language point to a desire on the part of the offended person to change the past. However, the past can never be changed—and it can never be made any better. Instead, the best an offended person can do is let the past be and move on.

This understanding that the past cannot be changed is the starting point in understanding the meaning of forgiveness. If one has to forgive, one has to first and foremost give up any hope of experiencing a better past and instead focus on making the future better. Forgiveness could be described—at least in part—as surrendering all hopes for a better past. As long as people make the conscious decision to live in the past in spite of other adverse outcomes or implications associated with it, they cannot experience forgiveness. In arguing so, it is appreciated that there is a clear distinction between forgiving and forgetting (or between forgiveness and forgetfulness). As was noted before, one of the greatest misconceptions regarding forgiveness—and one that has been responsible for many instances of refusal or failure to forgive—is that forgiving has to be followed by the forgetting of the offense. The reality is that human nature is such that it is often difficult for the mind to forget certain things, especially those that are hurtful or that pose a threat to the individual. This is part of the survival instinct of every human being.

Human beings were created to be able to flee from or fight out of dangerous situations they find themselves in. The mind keeps records of people, places, things, and events that are dangerous or that have the potential to pose a danger. The memory is designed to be used for purely survival reasons. Therefore, the ability of a human being to recall a nasty or uncomfortable event or situation is innate, and there is almost nothing anyone can do to change this reality. Just as one person will remember to keep away from a dangerous animal or place, perhaps due to past harm caused by the animal or location, the person will remember the person who hurt them and will be inclined toward wanting to avoid the person.[46] Therefore, it is not a failure to expect an offended person to forget about the incident and the person who hurt them even if forgiveness has taken place. The problem comes when the offended person makes it their responsibility to live in the memory of the hurt. At that point, the memory of the experience is harmful.

Science says is that forgiveness has nothing to do with forgetting the incident, person, or effect of the offense, but that is not necessarily the view of the Bible. The Bible does not explicitly require offended people to forget about the offense. Instead, it merely requires them to forgive without any preconditions. The scripture asks people to remember the fact that they have not forgiven and not to forget the fact that they have forgiven. Jesus taught his disciples:

> Therefore if thou bring thy gift to the altar, and there rememberest that thy brother hath ought against thee; Leave there thy gift before the altar, and go thy way; first be reconciled to thy brother, and then come and offer thy gift.[47]

Therefore, when it comes to forgiving, the emphasis has to be on remembering to forgive and not necessarily on attempting to forget the experience.

However, the Bible also says, "Their sins and lawless acts. I will remember no more."[48] This refers to the forgetting of the sins or offenses of human believers. It means that God will forgive the sins of the people and not have to remember anything about them. This verse points to forgiving and forgetting sins, yet it has to be kept in mind that God has the power and ability to forgive and forget. This is unique to him because he is all-knowing. No human being can purport to forgive and forget sins.

---

[46] Alistair McFadyen and Marcel Sarot, *Forgiveness and Truth* (Edinburgh, New York: T&T Clark, 2001), 21.

[47] Matthew 5:23–24 KJV.

[48] Hebrews 10:17 NIV.

## Focusing on What Forgiveness Is and Not on What Forgiveness Does

Many are the times when people seem to think of forgiveness in terms of what it does as opposed to what it is.[49] These are two different issues about forgiveness. The meaning of forgiveness has nothing to do with its outcomes—just as the result of forgiveness has nothing to do with the definition. Therefore, when seeking to understand the true meaning of forgiveness, one has to endeavor to ensure that the outcomes (what forgiveness does) are not allowed to alter that meaning. Yet the most common response that people tend to give when asked about the meaning of forgiveness is to begin by saying that forgiveness is "a process that ..." Such a response focuses on the outcomes of forgiveness and not forgiveness itself.

Forgiveness may, in some way, also be associated with its outcomes, but the two are different. It is also common for people to answer the question about forgiveness by citing its essence or nature. This is also wrong as it only describes forgiveness but does not define it or state its meaning. Unfortunately, even scholars and people who have dealt with issues of forgiveness and unforgiveness on a firsthand basis find it hard to explain what forgiveness means. Instead, they can go on and on about everything else about forgiveness but not its state or say what it means. Preachers talk and preach about forgiveness, and students read about it. This is why forgiveness tends to be portrayed or regarded more as a feeling than an act.

If forgiveness were a feeling, many people would long have died because of not having been forgiven and having to face the ultimate consequence of sin, namely death. This is because many people hardly ever feel that they have been forgiven their sins through the seemingly simple act of Jesus dying on the cross and nailing their sins on that cross. The fact of the matter is that Christ's death on the cross was not a simple thing. The act of forgiving is not simple. The reality is that when a person's sins or offenses have been forgiven, the person may never feel anything. Instead, forgiveness is based on God's promises. If there is any feeling at all, perhaps

---

[49] Everett L. Worthington Jr, *Handbook of Forgiveness* (Abingdon, United Kingdom: Routledge, 2007), 28.

it would be the feeling of inner peace that results from the deliberate choice to release the offender from the expectations that he or she would ever be able to make amends for the hurt or offense caused. Otherwise, forgiveness is not a feeling. An offending person is either forgiven or not regardless of how one feels about it. Similarly, a person knows—not feels—when they have been forgiven.

## Forgiveness as a Promise

One of the issues that the Bible is clear about is that forgiving an offender for their sins is a promise not to remember the offense. Whenever God forgave, he made a promise not to remember the sins against those forgiven: "your sins will I remember no more."

Without a promise to not remember sins, there would be no forgiveness. However, this ought not to mean that forgiveness means forgetting the sin. It is only God who cannot remember sin anymore once the sin is forgiven. As long as the sin remains, God remembers it, but as soon as God forgives the sin, then God can be expected not to remember the sin anymore. Therefore, it can be argued that at least when it comes to God's forgiveness of the sins of the world, forgiveness is a promise. It is a promise made not to remember sin forever. Subsequently, it can be argued that as long as God cannot remember one's sins, then forgiveness has taken place, or there has been forgiveness.

It is essential to add that God is all-knowing and all-powerful, and as such, he can do whatever he wants. This includes being able to remember anything he chooses to remember. This seems to contradict the view that forgiveness is a promise by God to not remember sin. The word *remember* as used in this context may not necessarily be the opposite in meaning (antonym) of the word *forget*. The reality is that God cannot forget anything. After all, he created everything—and forgetting anything would be unlike his nature.

However, just because God chooses not to remember sin does not mean that he cannot forget. God does not forget anything. Still, he is capable of not remembering sin. The first act (forgetting) is passive, while the second (not remembering) is active. By not remembering the sins of humanity, God makes the deliberate promise that he is determined to not sin by not remembering. God effectively promises to not bring up these matters to those who have been forgiven in days to come. Instead, he makes the promise to conceal or bury them someplace where they cannot be uncovered and used against the forgiven people. Therefore, forgiving is promising not to use the offense against the person in the future.[50] However, this is what many people seem to do. Even after claiming to have forgiven, they still get angry or bitter at the person in the future. As long as there are such manifestations, the person cannot be said to have truly forgiven.

Forgiveness cannot be said to have taken place or happened because there is no genuine promise not to remember. Even if a pledge to not remember is made, it becomes void when it cannot be kept. Since God is faithful and does not lie, he can be trusted to keep whatever promises he makes. This includes the promise to not remember sins. However, human beings in their fallen nature are prone to promising and not honoring the promises they make. This could explain why many people hardly ever forgive—even though they think they have forgiven. It also explains why forgiveness never really takes place in many situations where it is assumed or expected that forgiveness has taken place.

## Forgiveness as Dismissal of Owed Debt

Forgiveness could be described merely as the act of an offended person pardoning someone who has offended them.[51] Forgiveness has everything to do with pardoning because forgiveness is a term derived from the Greek word that means or translates into "letting go," which happens when a creditor does not demand to be paid an unpaid debt. In this regard, the owed person (the creditor) forgives or pardons the indebtedness of the debtor, and the debtor is no longer obligated to pay the debt. This analogy is arguably best illustrated in Jesus's lesson on prayer in what has come to be widely known as the Lord's Prayer. In the prayer, Jesus taught his disciples to pray to God by saying, "Forgive us our sins, for we also forgive

---

[50] Alistair McFadyen and Marcel Sarot, *Forgiveness and Truth* (Edinburgh, New York: T&T Clark, 2001), 9.
[51] Everett L. Worthington Jr., *Handbook of Forgiveness* (Abingdon, United Kingdom: Routledge, 2007), 12.

everyone who sins against us."[52] Jesus also used the same analogy in the parable of the slave who was without mercy, where forgiving was portrayed as being equal to the cancellation of a debt:

> And his fellowservant fell down at his feet, and besought him, saying, Have patience with me, and I will pay thee all. And he would not: but went and cast him into prison, till he should pay the debt. So when his fellowservants saw what was done, they were very sorry, and came and told unto their lord all that was done. Then his lord, after that he had called him, said unto him, O thou wicked servant, I forgave thee all that debt, because thou desiredst me: Shouldest, not thou also have had compassion on thy fellowservant, even as I had pity on thee? And his lord was wroth, and delivered him to the tormentors, till he should pay all that was due unto him. So likewise shall my heavenly Father do also unto you, if ye from your hearts forgive not every one his brother their trespasses.[53]

There is no doubt that this parable makes it clear what Jesus meant by forgiveness or forgiving. To understand the meaning of forgiveness, a careful and critical examination of this parable of the unmerciful servant is needed. The central message in the parable is the need for people to forgive because they have also been forgiven. Jesus expects that if people do not forgive their offenders for anything else, then they need to forgive them because they have also been forgiven of their offenses. From Jesus, this is the least that can be expected of anyone. Indeed, it is human nature to want to pay back for whatever has been done to us. When someone does something, good people are naturally inclined to do good to the person as a form of paying back even though such repayment is usually not expected.

People ought to repay those who offended them with forgiveness— just as they have been offered forgiveness. Jesus must have reasoned that because "all have sinned, and come short of the glory of God,"[54] they have

---

[52] Luke 11:4 NIV.
[53] Matthew 18:29–35 KJV.
[54] Romans 3:23 KJV.

at one time or another needed to be forgiven. Therefore, he wanted them to feel obligated to forgive, just as they have been forgiven. Indeed, every human being was forgiven when, if not anywhere else, Jesus died on the cross for the cleansing of all sin:

> But God commendeth his love toward us, in that, while
> we were yet sinners, Christ died for us.[55]

The attitude that Jesus expects all believers to have is that because the Son of Man died for them on the cross for the forgiveness of their sins, they have to forgive all those who sin against them similarly.

Unfortunately, many people are like the unmerciful servant who insisted on not forgiving his fellow servants for smaller or minor offenses even though his master had forgiven him for an even bigger offense. They quickly forget that they benefitted from someone else's kindness and forgiveness and want to withhold the same from those who offend them. On the contrary, it is expected that all people let go of their resentment and surrender whatever claims to be compensated they may have against or over the offender for the loss or hurt suffered.

Forgiveness happens when there is a letting go of the claims to be paid or restituted. It occurs when the offended person makes the deliberate decision not to claim what is otherwise seemingly due to them. In the case of the unmerciful servant, the master had the right to send the servant to prison—where the servant would have suffered irreparable harm. However, he chose to forego all claims. On the contrary, the servant insisted on getting whatever was owed to him and made claims to be compensated by his fellow servants. This was even though the servants begged him to let them go.

The Bible also teaches that true forgiveness is based on unselfish love:

> Love is patient, love is kind. It does not envy, it does not
> boast, it is not proud. It does not dishonor others, it is not
> self-seeking, it is not easily angered, it keeps no record of
> wrongs. Love does not delight in evil but rejoices with

---

[55] Romans 5:8 KJV.

the truth. It always protects, always trusts, always hopes, always perseveres. [56]

It can be argued that there are two types or forms of forgiveness portrayed in the Bible. The first one is where God forgives the sins of humankind by sending his only begotten Son, Jesus Christ, to die on the cross. The main goal of the mission, according to the Bible, is not to condemn the world but to save it:

> For God so loved the world, that he gave his only begotten Son, that whosoever believeth in him should not perish, but have everlasting life. For God sent not his Son into the world to condemn the world; but that the world through him might be saved.[57]

This biblical text brings to the fore two essential things about forgiveness: love and giving. For forgiveness to take place or be possible, the Bible seems to suggest that there has to be love followed by giving. As was noted before, forgiveness is based on unconditional love since one cannot forgive unless one has love and respect for the offender and love and respect for God. When people love God, they will be able to love their neighbors and therefore be in a position to forgive their neighbors when they are offended:

> We love him, because he first loved us. If a man say, I love God, and hateth his brother, he is a liar: for he that loveth not his brother whom he hath seen, how can he love God whom he hath not seen? And this commandment have we from him, That he who loveth God love his brother also.[58]

Therefore, loving God has to be commensurate with loving one's brother. This, in turn, means that God expects his people to always be in a state of love with their brothers or neighbors. God expects that people

---

[56]  1 Corinthians 13:4–7 NIV.
[57]  John 3:16–17 KJV.
[58]  1 John 4:19–21 KJV.

will always have a love for one another at every time and in every situation. This paves the way for forgiveness because, without love, it is not possible to forgive. When people are in a continuous state of love with God and with one another, they can forgive without any preconditions. The love that one has for the other person (the offender) will result in the offended person letting go of their resentment and surrender or giving up whatever claims to be compensated they may have against or over the offender for the loss or hurt suffered. Therefore, love ultimately leads to giving, and this underscores the importance of the two in the process of forgiving.

Therefore, the second form of forgiving is that where human beings should forgive other people (those who the people invariably recover to as brothers or neighbors). The identity of these people is not as important as their need for forgiveness. The terms "brothers" and "neighbors" as used in the Bible refer to those people around the offended person who may need to be forgiven.

As long as people are still in the world, they will continue hurting each other and needing to forgive and be forgiven just as they keep sinning against God and having to seek God's forgiveness. The good news is that even though humans will experience many problems in this world that will take away their peace, there is hope because Jesus overcame the world. Therefore, all people can be expected to overcome all kinds of sin and temptations—just as Jesus did:

> These things I have spoken unto you, that in me ye might
> have peace. In the world ye shall have tribulation: but be
> of good cheer; I have overcome the world.[59]

This Bible verse has often been used concerning temptations and not necessarily in the context of forgiveness. However, the tendency not to forgive is arguably one of the most challenging and enduring attractions human beings ever face. Few other commands are as hard to keep and obey than God's command for people to forgive those who sin against them. As the parable of the unmerciful servant illustrates, it is human nature to want to be repaid or compensated for whatever claims they

---

[59] John 16:33 KJV.

may have against other people. Usually, human beings want to be paid or compensated in full and not partially; this more often than not results in a refusal to forgive. Even if there is forgiveness, it is often more of a struggle than something that flows naturally out of love for the offender.

When God chose to forgive humankind of their sins, he did so entirely and not partially. That is why he had to use the ultimate sacrificial Lamb—his only begotten Son. God realized that as even though the sacrificial blood of bulls and lambs was required under the Law of Moses, it was not sufficient to cleanse humanity of all sin and for eternity. Instead, the blood of lambs and bulls would only cleanse for a limited period. That is why repeated sacrifices needed to be offered:

> The law is only a shadow of the good things that are coming—not the realities themselves. For this reason it can never, by the same sacrifices repeated endlessly year after year, make perfect those who draw near to worship. Otherwise, would they not have stopped being offered? For the worshipers would have been cleansed once for all, and would no longer have felt guilty for their sins. But those sacrifices are an annual reminder of sins. It is impossible for the blood of bulls and goats to take away sins.[60]

Only through the blood of Jesus Christ was it possible for all sins to be washed forever so that the former sinner would never again have to need to be forgiven for their sins from time to time. Therefore, Jesus effectively did for humanity what bulls and lambs could not do: becoming the ultimate sacrificial Lamb whose blood does not cleanse only partially but cleanses eternally. That is why the psalmist said regarding the coming Messiah:

> Sacrifice and offering you did not desire—but my ears you have opened—burnt offerings and sin offerings you did not require. Then I said, "Here I am, I have come—it

---

[60] Hebrews 10:1–4 NIV.

is written about me in the scroll. I desire to do your will,
my God; your law is within my heart."[61]

This, in turn, means that sacrifices were required in the days of the
Law of Moses, but they were no longer needed because they were set aside
by the coming of Jesus.

In the same way, it is now possible for every human being to be
forgiven for their offenses as the ultimate price for sin was already paid
on Calvary's cross. Whatever remains is for human beings to forgive their
brothers just as God forgave them. The difference is that God's forgiveness
of the sins of the world was not obligatory because it came from his love
for the world:

> For God so loved the world, that he gave his only begotten
> Son, that whosoever believeth in him should not perish,
> but have everlasting life.[62]

On the contrary, human beings are under obligation from God to
forgive. They have no option but to forgive. If they do not forgive, there
are consequences:

> If you forgive other people when they sin against you,
> your heavenly Father will also forgive you. But if you do
> not forgive others their sins, your Father will not forgive
> your sins."[63]

Because God had to pay so high a price—in fact, the highest price
possible—for the forgiveness of sin, he does not expect anyone not to
forgive. The blood of his Son that was shed on the cross at Calvary seems
to be the constant reminder that sin always has to be forgiven—and that
there is no room for lack of forgiveness whatsoever. Jesus himself declared,

---

[61] Psalm 40:6–8 NIV.
[62] John 3:16 NIV.
[63] Matthew 6:14–15 NIV.

"This is my blood of the covenant, which is poured out for many for the forgiveness of sins."[64]

Such a heavy price was paid by Jesus not just so that human beings can be forgiven by God but also by fellow human beings. In the same way, the same blood was shed to make it possible for forgiveness to follow from every human being to all others who need forgiveness. Jesus could be said to have served as the perfect example of forgiveness by agreeing to offer his own life for the forgiveness of sin.

Fortunately for human beings, God does not require us to give up the lives of those we love to get forgiveness. All we need to do is decide in our hearts not to continue expecting our debts to be paid by those people who we believe owe us for the hurt or suffering caused.

In essence, forgiveness ought not to be any more difficult if people were to heed his exhortation:

> Consider him that endured such contradiction of sinners against himself, lest ye be wearied and faint in your minds. Ye have not yet resisted unto blood, striving against sin.[65]

At the very least, it would have been a significant struggle for human beings to forgive sins or to forgive those who offended them if this required the shedding of the blood of their loved ones (let alone themselves). This could explain why God, in his infinite wisdom, chose to offer Jesus as the sacrificial lamb so that human beings would not keep offering sacrifices regularly or every time they sinned and needed to be forgiven. Instead, Jesus's blood paid for all sin once and for all. This is how important God regards the issue of forgiveness, and it is no wonder that he expects no less from human beings when it comes to forgiveness: they have to forgive without any conditions just as he forgave them without zany situations.

To further show that God gives a lot of priority to the issue of forgiveness, he said he does not just expect human beings to forgive those who sin against them a few times or for small, minor offenses and not the significant offenses. Instead, he expects forgiveness as many times as there will be people in need of being forgiven. This was made evident in

---

[64] Matthew 26:28 NIV.
[65] Hebrews 12:3–4 KJV.

Jesus's response to Peter's question: "Lord, how often shall my brother sin against me, and I forgive him? Up to seven times?"[66] Jesus, wonderfully and without a second thought, said, "I do not say to you, up to seven times, but up to seventy times seven."[67]

Peter's question illustrates the dominant and usual human approach to and view of the whole issue of forgiveness. On the other hand, Jesus's response illustrates God's perception of the importance of forgiveness. On their part, human beings have a view of forgiveness as being conditional, short term, and with a limited lifespan. However, God expects forgiveness to be something that is continuous, unconditional, and without a specific time frame. God wants forgiveness not to be something that happens in limited circumstances or for a specific period of time; he wants it to go on endlessly.

Peter expected Jesus to agree with him that a sinful neighbor should only be forgiven a maximum of seven times, after which there would be no need to forgive any more (or any longer). After all, this is the usual human reasoning. For human beings, some people need not be forgiven—at least seven times—because they are too arrogant, have refused to acknowledge their mistakes, have not sought forgiveness, do not understand or appreciate the gravity of their offense, or have some other excuse. There is a reason to believe that Peter thought seven times was way too many for him and his colleagues. Seven is the number of completion or perfection, and by implying that those who sin against others should be forgiven seven times, Peter must have thought this was the absolute maximum.

However, God's view of and attitude toward forgiveness is markedly different from that of humans. Rather than agree with Peter, Jesus raises the standard beyond the wildest expectations of his audience by saying that forgiveness has to be done seventy times seven. It would take a selfish person to keep a record of that many forgiven wrongs before running out of memory. Jesus may have intended to illustrate that forgiveness has to be limitless and not tied to any number of situations. He must have reasoned that even if someone could keep good records of wrongdoing

---

[66] Matthew 18:21 KJV.
[67] Matthew 18:22 NIV.

and forgiving, they would never amount to seventy times seven (whatever Jesus meant by that).

Therefore, forgiveness could be described as the act of dismissing debt. This kind of dismissal of debt is specifically illustrated throughout the New Testament using the term *aphesis,* which is a Greek noun that denotes "dismissal" or "release." This means that when an offended person forgives, he or she effectively dismisses the debt owed to them by the offender. This is the debt of having been hurt or harmed. On the other hand, the offended person's debt is dismissed when the person is forgiven. Forgiving is, in this regard, the act of rejecting the debt from the offender's thoughts and not necessarily in the physical realm. For instance, if the offender owes money, the money may still need to be repaid even after the act of forgiving takes place in the heart and not in the physical realm.

It takes a person who has genuinely forgiven their offenders for loving one's enemies and even praying for them. This is in line with Jesus's command to "love your enemies, do good to those who hate you."[68] To be able to love one's enemies, one has to be willing and ready to forgo any debts these people owe them. This is why love is almost always a prerequisite for forgiveness. Without love in general and love for the offender in particular, it would be difficult or even impossible to forgive one's offenders.

## Forgiveness as Dismissing Demands that Others Owe

Forgiveness could also be said to be the dismissal of the demand that others owe a person something. This is especially so if the debtors fail to meet the expectations of the offended person or do not keep a promise or treat one in a just manner. This is a kind of forgiveness that could be illustrated by Jesus's command: "If someone strikes you on the right cheek, turn to him the other also."[69] This command did not go down well with the disciples listening to Jesus teach.

Under normal circumstances, human nature demands that when one person strikes another, the first person needs to reciprocate in kind. This was somewhat even legal in the Old Testament, where it was a tooth for a tooth and an eye for an eye. The Law of Moses made specific

---

[68] Luke 6:27 NIV.
[69] Matthew 5:39 NIV.

demands for people who committed individual acts of sin, and these often included being given punishments that were equal in measure to the offense committed. The more serious the offense, the harsher the penalty that would be given.

This practice changed with the coming of Jesus. Paul said, "Therefore, if anyone is in Christ, the new creation has come: The old has gone, the new is here!"[70]

As a result of the coming of a new dispensation (Jesus Christ and the grace of God taking over the place of the Law), there was no more extended room for people to repay others for their evil. Instead, the forgiveness of sins became the norm. It was within this context that Jesus required those struck on the right cheek also to offer the left one to be hit as well:

> But I say to you who hear, love your enemies, do good to those who hate you, bless those who curse you, pray for those who abuse you. To one who strikes you on the cheek, offer the other also, and from one who takes away your cloak do not withhold your tunic either. Give to everyone who begs from you, and from one who takes away your goods do not demand them back. And as you wish that others would do to you, do so to them.[71]

This is arguably one of the best illustrations of forgiveness. It is about choosing not to demand something from another person who is otherwise rightly due to one or justified. A person who is struck by another is justified in feeling angry at the offender and possibly even striking back. However, forgiveness is when the struck person chooses not to strike back.

The analogy also extends to the issue of someone taking one's coat against the will of the coat's owner. Rather than the offended person getting angry, repaying the offense by taking the offender's coat in retaliation, or taking some other punitive measure, he or she chooses to let the offender take the coat and offers the offender his or her own cloak as well. This could be said to be going beyond what is expected of one. Instead of trying

---

[70] 2 Corinthians 5:17 NIV.
[71] Luke 6:27–31 ESV.

to reclaim the coat that has been taken forcibly, the offended person offers the offender a cloak in addition to the coat.

Jesus taught that it is only by not repaying evil for evil but repaying evil with good that the people of the world would indeed come to understand the kingdom of God. This was a kingdom that functioned based on principles that were unlike any of the beliefs and customs of the world.

Paul also made it clear that when people do what is kind to those who seek to hurt them or who do wrong to them, they are piling coals of fire on their very heads:

> Therefore if thine enemy hunger, feed him; if he thirst, give him drink: for in so doing thou shalt heap coals of fire on his head.[72]

## Forgiveness as a Deliberate Choice

Even though this may not have been mentioned before among the misconceptions of forgiveness, many people falsely think or assume that forgiving is something that one feels. As a result, it is common for people to say that they do not feel like forgiving or that they are not in the mood to forgive someone. The reality is that forgiveness is not a feeling but a choice that the offended person deliberately makes. Feelings come and go depending on the situations people find themselves in and the prevailing circumstances. For instance, a person can feel happy at one point in time but sad at another point in time. People may also feel like doing something at one point in time and not doing the same thing at some other point. For instance, a person may feel like eating food in the morning and during the evening. However, the same person may not feel like eating during the night. These feelings cannot be attributed to forgiving or forgiveness because forgiveness is not a feeling.

The choice to forgive often entails having the offended person make the deliberate decision or choice to go before God—possibly on one's knees—and ask God to empower them to forgive. This is out of the realization that forgiving is difficult, and one may not be able to do it

---

[72] Romans 12:20 KJV.

with their power or using their strength. Instead, they have to rely on the enabling and unlimited power of God. A person who wants to eat needs not ask God for such power since eating can be accomplished relatively easily as long as there is food. This is why forgiving is far from a feeling.

Forgiveness is also a choice to let go of the negative thoughts of hatred and animosity in one's heart. An offended person hardly ever thinks of things or issues other than the fact that he or she has been hurt deeply. To be able to think about anything different, the person has to exert a lot of effort and subdue the dominant thoughts of having been injured or harmed by the offender. Because offended people dwell too much on these negative thoughts to leave enough room for other neutral or positive thoughts, they hardly ever, if at all, think about anything else other than the hurt. The longer they refuse to forgive, the less likely they are to think of anything else—and the more they become trapped in a vicious cycle of negative emotions, bitterness, and rage. These thoughts can grip a person to the extent that they take over every aspect of the person from thinking to acting. Since thoughts precede actions, the negative feelings of revenge, hatred, anger, and rage tend to result in largely negative works.

The offended person may, therefore, exhibit negative behavioral traits such as hurting other people and not respecting authority. A person who is hurting as a result of not forgiving will hurt all people around them as the bottled-up negative emotions can only lead to negative behaviors:

> O generation of vipers, how can ye, being evil, speak good things? For out of the abundance of the heart, the mouth speaketh.[73]

The mouths of offended people who have refused to forgive pour out equally hurting words designed to injure. The problem is that they injure people who had no role to play in the offense or who knew nothing about the offense.

When an offended person makes the rational choice to forgive, the negative thoughts and hatred that are bottled up in their hearts get released, and the person can live more comfortably and feel more relaxed.

---

[73] Matthew 12:34 KJV.

It is akin to getting a heavy burden off one's chest or head and being able to walk around faster and more efficiently. An offended person cannot "feel" or wish away these thoughts of hatred. They have to choose to let the thoughts go upon the realization that holding onto them only makes matters worse for them. It is when people decide to let go of these negative emotions and feelings that they can be truly free.[74]

Because the negative thoughts and feelings make the offended person practically sick and unwell, letting them go helps them calm down and, by extension, increases their levels of happiness and significantly improves their health:

> A heart at peace gives life to the body, but envy rots the bones.[75]

Forgiving is also choosing to go to God to be helped and comforted rather than having to dwell on past wrongs and offenses. This is important as it is often done in spite of the concerned people's feelings to the contrary. Usually, the offended people would not feel like seeking help—not even help from God who is all-knowing. They will also not feel like asking to be comforted by God and God's Word. Instead, their predominant feeling seems to be maintaining the status quo and doing nothing about it. Offended people sometimes feel like replaying the offense in their minds over and over as a way of reminding themselves of how severe or hurtful the offense was. Therefore, they can never get help or comfort through feelings but via a deliberate choice to seek advice.

The biblical meaning of forgiveness is not different from that used by psychologists. In psychology, forgiveness denotes a conscious as well as a deliberate choice to let go of the negative feelings of revenge and resentment toward a person who has hurt someone often concerning whether the person deserves to be forgiven or not."[76] This definition also emphasizes the aspect of consciousness and deliberate decision. These are

---

[74] Everett L. Worthington Jr., *Handbook of Forgiveness* (Abingdon, United Kingdom: Routledge, 2007), 27.
[75] Proverbs 14:30 NIV.
[76] Everett L. Worthington Jr., *Handbook of Forgiveness* (Abingdon, United Kingdom: Routledge, 2007), 11.

not the only essential ingredients of forgiveness, but they are among the most important. Forgiveness cannot happen unless and until there is a careful and conscious decision on the part of the offended person to let go of the feelings of vengeance and resentment toward the offender. If there is no deliberate decision, then it may appear as though forgiveness has taken place when, in fact, it has not. For instance, if a person is forced to forgive another person for the unity of a team or group to be preserved or maintained, the offended person may only have the appearance of having forgiven. In reality, though, the person may not have forgiven at all.

There is no question that if brethren are to live (and work) together in harmony as commanded by Jesus, they need to be ready to forgive each other. When brothers do not live in peace, there is chaos and all kinds of evil. Therefore, the common practice has been for church leaders to encourage—or even push—brethren to forgive each other so that the work of the ministries can go on. While this may look like an ethical and moral initiative, it has the effect of resulting in fake forgiveness where the offender only puts on the appearance of having forgiven when one has not. Forgiveness only happens when there is a deliberate decision by the offended person to let go of the feelings of vengeance and resentment.[77]

Forced forgiveness is often without deliberation and conscious decision-making. Instead, the offended person usually has no choice but to act based on what others tell them. The person is moved more by the need to preserve the relationship than by the conscious and deliberate choice to let go of the resentment and vengeance. As a result, the offended person may still harbor resentment and revenge in their heart even though they outwardly look and seem to have forgiven or let go of their bitterness and vengeance. They try as much as possible to conceal these negative feelings, especially when in the company of other brethren, but they can explode when they are in contact with the offender.

---

[77] F. LeRon Shults and Steven J. Sandage, *The Faces of Forgiveness: Searching for Wholeness and Salvation* (Grand Rapids, MI: Baker Academic, 2003), 47.

# CHAPTER 3

# THE CHRISTIAN MOTIVATION TO FORGIVE

As has already been noted, forgiving others (or even oneself) is one of life's most challenging and seemingly impossible tasks—regardless of whether the offense is relatively small or seriously damaging to the offended person. Forgiving is a complicated process, especially when the offended person has to forgive a person other than oneself. This explains why, more often than not, the process of forgiving others is long and sometimes problematic and even confrontational. If humankind had a way of circumventing forgiveness, then many would have chosen to avoid it rather than have to do it. Among believers, forgiving is no less difficult and challenging task,[78] and this is in spite of the incentive there often is to forgive.

## Why Christians Should Forgive

The Bible is explicit on why believers must forgive those who offend them. Even more important is that the Bible does not require base or peg forgiveness on anything so that people could only forgive based on certain conditions. That is why throughout the scripture, there are many teachings and lessons on forgiveness, but none of these is illustrated with conditional words such as "if," "unless," or "but." Instead, forgiveness is to be unconditional, as it is usually for the benefit of the offended person to forgive. Typically, people are expected to do things that are beneficial

---

[78] June Hunt, *Biblical Counseling Keys on Forgiveness: The Freedom to Let Go* (Dallas, TX: Hope for The Heart, 2008), 32.

to them. Therefore, there is enough motivation for people to forgive. However, many still grapple with it because they either fail to understand and appreciate its benefits to them, or they know the benefits but are not convinced that these benefits can genuinely accrue to them. As was noted before, Jesus is the exemplifier of unconditional forgiveness that could be said to have been motivated by the understanding that forgiving helps the offended person more than it does help (if at all) the offender.

On the cross, Jesus cried out, "Father, forgive them, they know not what they do."[79] Not much thought seems to have been given to those words, which were among the very last Jesus ever spoke. For instance, why did Jesus choose to forgive such vile men for an offense of such monumental magnitude? Only a few of the apostles managed to emulate Jesus's example in terms of forgiving even the most terrible of sins or offenses. Even the few who forgave seemingly terrible sins of offenses never needed to forgive people who killed them based on false testimony. Stephen did manage to ask God to forgive his killers:

> While they were stoning him, Stephen prayed, "Lord Jesus, receive my spirit." Then he fell on his knees and cried out, "Lord, do not hold this sin against them." When he had said this, he fell asleep.[80]

However, it can be argued that Stephen was at least getting killed based on some provable offense, namely preaching Jesus Christ.

On the contrary, Jesus was crucified based on the false accusation of claiming equality with God (blaspheming), which in reality, he never did. Jesus could not have claimed equality with God because he was God. A person does not claim to be equal to oneself. Even when one considers the Holy Trinity (where the Father has authority over the Son), Jesus could be said to have never claimed to be equal to the Father or even the Holy Spirit. Therefore, his crucifixion had no legal or moral basis. Yet he asked the Father to forgive his killers (meaning he had forgiven them as well). What motivated him to forgive?

---

[79] Luke 23:34 NIV.
[80] Acts 7:59–60 NIV.

The answer to this question can be found in the benefits of forgiving as Jesus understood and taught them. The first benefit is that forgiving does not in any way negate the pain suffered. If there has to be true forgiveness, then believers, in particular, have to understand that the act will not necessarily deny or minimize the pain suffered and the hurting endured. Jesus bore it all but still forgave. He must have realized that refusing to forgive would not in any way change the fact that he had been falsely accused of blasphemy and subsequently killed—and this not by just anyone but the very people who benefitted from his ministry the most (religious leaders and his apostle, Judas).

If there was to be justification for not forgiving, then Jesus had them all. Yet his understanding that forgiving is paramount regardless of the pain led him to do it under the most challenging circumstances—at the point of death on the cross. He did not do it for the sake—or to the benefit of—his offenders but for himself and what he stood for. He wanted to relieve himself of having to live with the burden brought about by thoughts of bitterness and hatred associated with being offended (exceptionally and significantly hurt).

Jesus, choosing to forgive his killers, had some benefits in mind for those who were persecuting him. Considering his saving mission on earth, Jesus may have chosen to forgive so that his killers could be saved and, therefore, not barred from entering the kingdom of God. However, Jesus did forgive for his benefit, which included being able to accomplish his mission on earth. Jesus's overarching and successful earthly mission to save the lost would have ended in disarray at that critical moment on the cross if he had refused to forgive his killers. By forgiving them, Jesus conveyed an essential message to both the killers and the onlookers that the kingdom to which Jesus belonged was one of peace and not violence. He showed that God has indeed relented in his anger against those who sinned against him and had, by grace, chosen to forgive everyone regardless of their sins:

> The Lord is merciful and gracious, slow to anger, and plenteous in mercy. He will not always chide: neither will

he keep his anger forever. He hath not dealt with us after our sins; nor rewarded us according to our iniquities.[81]

This had always been Jesus's central message while on earth. Jesus emphasized the unconditional nature of forgiveness throughout his earthly ministry, and this ministry would have ended up in disaster if Jesus had failed to forgive what could be considered the greatest sin of all time.

## Forgiving to Avoid Getting into Bondage

Another reason why people ought to be motivated to forgive is that failure to forgive comes with the risk of sending one to prison. A lot has already been said regarding how refusal to forgive is analogous to a self-imposed prison. In the parable of the wicked servant, the central message was that unless there is forgiveness, one risks being imprisoned. In a similar lesson, Jesus taught that refusing to forgive could land a person into prison—albeit indirectly:

> Therefore, if you are offering your gift at the altar and there remember that your brother or sister has something against you, leave your gift there in front of the altar. First, go and be reconciled to them; then come and offer your gift. "Settle matters quickly with your adversary who is taking you to court. Do it while you are still together on the way, or your adversary may hand you over to the judge, and the judge may hand you over to the officer, and you may be thrown into prison. Truly I tell you, you will not get out until you have paid the last penny."[82]

There may be disagreements regarding who Jesus was addressing in this passage—whether the offended person or the offender—but it matters little because, either way, the central message was about forgiveness and its importance. Jesus makes it clear that unless there is forgiveness, there is the likelihood of someone ending up in prison and having to undergo

---

[81] Psalm 103:8–10 KJV.
[82] Matthew 5:23–26 NIV.

suffering. Most of the time, the person who remembers that someone has something against them is indeed the offended person. It is therefore highly possible that Jesus was asking those who feel offended by others to give priority to getting reconciled—through forgiveness—instead of bringing offerings before God. In fact, in one of the biblical lessons in this regard, God says that he desires obedience more than sacrifice. That is why the prophet Samuel said:

> Does the Lord delight in burnt offerings and sacrifices
> as much as in obeying the Lord? To obey is better than
> sacrifice, and to heed is better than the fat of rams.[83]

God wants his people to obey his commandments, including this one:

> If you are offering your gift at the altar and there remember
> that your brother or sister has something against you,
> leave your gift there in front of the altar. First, go and be
> reconciled to them; then come and offer your gift.[84]

If God is more pleased when people forgive each other than if they offer him sacrifices, then this is a motivation to forgive. If for nothing else, brethren in particular need to forgive each other so that God may be pleased with them.[85] Many benefits come to a person when God is happy with them. These include hearing their prayers and making them his sons and daughters. When God said to Jesus, "This is my Son in whom I am much pleased," the message was accompanied by the outpouring of the Holy Spirit.

Moreover, God singles out those with whom he is displeased for punishment. Therefore, forgiving could be termed as one of the ways through which a person can avoid or escape God's wrath and subsequent punishment. Surely, it is much better to forgive than to refuse to forgive and attract God's wrath.

---

[83]  1 Samuel 15:22 NIV.

[84]  Matthew 5:23–24 NIV.

[85]  F. LeRon Shults and Steven J. Sandage, *The Faces of Forgiveness: Searching for Wholeness and Salvation* (Grand Rapids, MI: Baker Academic, 2003), 43.

It is also essential to add that, in reality, God values sacrifices offered to him by his people. The fact that he values forgiveness (which is an act of obedience) more than sacrifice underscores the importance of forgiveness to God. Throughout the Bible, the offering of sacrifices was one of the ways through which people would commune with God. Sacrifice preceded any communications between people and God in both the Old Testament and the New Testament. The only significant difference is that in the Old Testament, the sacrifices were of the blood of animals, and in the New Testament, the sacrifices were in the form of praises and thanksgiving to God. Therefore, it can be argued that failure to forgive can lead to God's rejection of one's sacrifices.

In the Old Testament, sacrifices were only accepted if the person offering them—through the high priest—was without sin (after being consecrated). Those with sin had their sacrifices rejected outright. The same was done in the New Testament; believers' prayers and praises are only acceptable before God if those offering them are blameless. Therefore, not forgiving—by being a sin before God—can prevent God's acceptance of one's sacrifices and, by extension, one's prayers. If prayers are to be unhindered, brethren have to make it a habit to forgive those who sin against then.

## Forgiving Fosters Harmonious and Peaceful Coexistence

One of the most memorable incidents that ever took place in the history of the world was Jesus's Crucifixion on the cross at Calvary. That event has remained edged in the minds of people for ages. Yet Jesus still managed to forgive his killers before he gave up his spirit on the cross. Even before being crucified, Jesus had endured some of the cruelest punishment ever meted out on anyone. They beat him up, forced him to carry his cross, spat on him, slapped him, and forced a crown made out of thorns on his head. The pain was, without a doubt, excruciating, yet Jesus did not get angry. If he ever got angry at all, he did not let his anger get the better of him:

> Jesus, when He was reviled, did not revile in return; when
> He suffered, He did not threaten but committed Himself
> to Him who judges righteously.[86]

For Christians, the answer to the age-old question on why forgiving is even worth considering lies right in what Jesus did as recorded in this verse as well as other verses about forgiveness.

Considering Jesus, who had to ensure so much at the hands of his tormentors but still forgave, one wonders why he did it. First, it can be argued that forgiveness is necessary for brethren to live together in harmony. Every time there is an offense, at least two people are separated by the offense committed. The offended person, in particular, does not want to see the offender or have anything to do with them. If Jesus had been human, he would have sworn never to set his feet in the sinful world again:

> He came unto his own, and his own received him not."[87]

Yet one of the promises he made regarding Jesus was that he would be back:

> Ye men of Galilee, why stand ye gazing up into heaven?
> This same Jesus, which is taken up from you into heaven,
> shall so come in like manner as ye have seen him go into
> heaven."[88]

> Peace I leave with you; my peace I give you. I do not
> give to you as the world gives. Do not let your hearts be
> troubled and do not be afraid.[89]

Even though Jesus was leaving the world, he was still concerned about the need for peace in the world. He did not want believers fighting among

---

[86] 1 Peter 2:23 NIV.
[87] John 1:11 KJV.
[88] Acts 1:11 KJV.
[89] John 14:27 KJV.

themselves or with nonbelievers. Instead, he wanted them to live together in harmony:

> Behold, how good and how pleasant it is for brethren to dwell together in unity! It is like the precious oil upon the head, running down on the beard, the beard of Aaron, Running down on the edge of his garments. It is like the dew of Hermon, Descending upon the mountains of Zion; for there, the Lord commanded the blessing—Life forevermore.[90]

Through forgiveness, believers can live together in harmony.[91] Jesus understood that as long as people were in the world, they would face many tribulations. As a result, they would offend others and God and also get offended. Therefore, he wanted them to make forgiveness part of their daily lives. That could explain why he demonstrated one of the greatest acts of forgiveness by forgiving those who had hurt him deeply. It is only to the extent that believers can emulate Christ in forgiving others that they can genuinely be Christlike. Being Christlike has to include offering unconditional forgiveness. This means that Christians have to forgive when it is convenient for them *and* even when it is not suitable or when it does not make sense.

If anyone had just reason not to forgive, then it was Jesus because he was crucified even though he was without sin:

> For he hath made him be sin for us, who knew no sin; that we might be made the righteousness of God in him.[92]

All Christians have sinned, and it would be somehow right if they were offended or persecuted. Jesus had no such sin:

---

[90] Psalm 133:1–3 NKJV.
[91] Derek Prince, *The Three Most Powerful Words: Discovering the Freedom of Releasing the Ones Who Hurt Us* (Charlotte, NC: Derek Prince Ministries, 2006), 15.
[92] 2 Corinthians 5:21 KJV.

But he was wounded for our transgressions, he was bruised
for our iniquities: the chastisement of our peace was upon
him, and with his stripes, we are healed.[93]

Forgiving is the duty and obligation of every Christians because Jesus
wanted it to be so.

## Forgiving in Order to Be Forgiven by God

There are many commands in the Bible, but one of the most outstanding
is the command to forgive. Throughout the scripture, God commands
his people to forgive those who sin against them even as their sins have
been forgiven. Therefore, one of the reasons Christians have to forgive is
that they have also been exonerated or they also need to be forgiven. The
message in this regard is clear. As long as anyone has ever needed to be
forgiven or will ever need to be forgiven, then they also have to forgive.
That is how simple the command to forgive demands. Because all have
sinned and fall short of the glory of God, no one can say that they cannot
forgive. Everyone must forgive—just as God forgave.

The parable of the unmerciful servant best illustrates this attitude.
The servant had been forgiven by his master of a debt owed. However,
he turned around and threatened to throw his fellow servants into prison
if they did not repay him. Even though they begged him for mercy,
he remained adamant and insisted on being paid his debt. It took the
intervention of the master to bring some sense into the unmerciful servant
by also threatening to throw him in prison for the forgiven debt:

And his fellowservant fell down at his feet, and besought
him, saying, Have patience with me, and I will pay thee
all. And he would not: but went and cast him into prison,
till he should pay the debt. So when his fellowservants
saw what was done, they were very sorry, and came and
told unto their lord all that was done. Then his lord, after
that he had called him, said unto him, O thou wicked
servant, I forgave thee all that debt, because thou desiredst

---

[93] Isaiah 53:5 KJV.

me: Shouldest, not thou also have had compassion on thy fellowservant, even as I had pity on thee? And his lord was wroth, and delivered him to the tormentors, till he should pay all that was due unto him. So likewise shall my heavenly Father do also unto you, if ye from your hearts forgive not every one his brother their trespasses.[94]

This is the same attitude that Christians ought to have concerning forgiveness. They have to forgive because they have been forgiven. Unless they forgive, their heavenly Father will also not forgive them. This is something God made clear:

So likewise shall my heavenly Father do also unto you, if ye from your hearts forgive not every one his brother their trespasses.[95]

This implies that if Christians cannot find any other reason to forgive, then they are obligated to forgive because God has forgiven them—or God will forgive them when (not if) they sin. Some people have argued that they ought not to be made to forgive when they do not feel like forgiving. This is a valid argument, no doubt, but it is also a misconceived one. God did not suggest that believers forgive those who sin against them. He commanded them to forgive. Therefore, it takes someone who does not honor and fear God to argue that they do not feel like forgiving.

Moreover, forgiveness is not a feeling. It is a deliberate choice someone makes irrespective of one's emotions.[96] If people forgave based on their beliefs, the world would be full of hatred and evil because no one would be willing or ready to forgive. Forgiveness is difficult, which could explain why God made it mandatory as opposed to optional. Jesus must not have felt like forgiving his accusers and killers, especially given that he knew deep down—and he had many witnesses—that he had done no evil and

---

[94] Matthew 18:29–35 KJV.
[95] Matthew 18: 35 KJV.
[96] F. LeRon Shults and Steven J. Sandage, *The Faces of Forgiveness: Searching for Wholeness and Salvation* (Grand Rapids, MI: Baker Academic, 2003), 40.

that his accusers had no evidence. Still, he went ahead and forgave them in spite of the feelings. Similarly, Christians always have to forgive.

When forgiving, Christians need to have the attitude of Christ who, being gripped with fear, said, "Father, if thou be willing, remove this cup from me: nevertheless not my will, but thine, be done."[97] This means that Christians are to admit that it is difficult to forgive and that they do not feel like doing it. However, they also have to be willing to surrender their will to God's will.

God's will is for every Christian to forgive everyone, irrespective of how one feels about it. It is right of every offender to be forgiven when they sin:

> When you stand praying if you hold anything against anyone, forgive him, so that your Father in heaven may forgive you your sins.[98]

Forgiveness begets forgiveness, and unforgiveness begets unforgiveness. This sounds more like the Old Testament practice—where every sin receives its full punishment as prescribed by the law—but there is a significant difference, which is that even if someone decides not to forgive, no specific penalty is set out on them. Instead, they are left at the mercy of God, and he decides what to do.

Because God is merciful, many people have been able to get away with unforgiveness for a long time; this has tended to encourage many others not to forgive. However, God's patience will someday wear thin, and his wrath will be unleashed. That is why he says that he will not contend with sin forever:

> And the Lord said, My spirit shall not always strive with man, for that he also is flesh: yet his days shall be a hundred and twenty years.[99]

---

[97] Luke 22:42 KJV.
[98] Mark 11:25 NIV.
[99] Genesis 6:3 KJV.

God has the power to do anything to anyone who does not heed God's commands, and this includes being killed by God. It may seem out of place and even out of God's character to kill someone for failing to forgive. The reality is that before God, there is no greater or lesser sin. Instead, all sins are equal and attract punishment. The truth is that God hates sin. Therefore, his mercy and grace ought not to be used as an excuse for people to sin.

Paul made it clear that people ought not to sin so that grace may abound even more:

> What shall we say then? Shall we continue in sin, that grace may abound? God forbid. How shall we, that are dead to sin, live any longer therein? Know ye not, that so many of us as were baptized into Jesus Christ were baptized into his death? Therefore we are buried with him by baptism into death: that like as Christ was raised up from the dead by the glory of the Father, even so, we also should walk in newness of life.[100]

Even if those who refuse to forgive escape God's wrath here on earth, they will not escape it on the Day of Judgment:

> Because of their wickedness, do not let them escape; in your anger, God brings the nations down.[101]

> For the wrath of God is revealed from heaven against all ungodliness and unrighteousness of men, who hold the truth in unrighteousness.[102]

---

[100] Romans 6:1–4 KJV.

[101] Psalm 56:7 NIV.

[102] Romans 1:18 KJV.

## Forgiveness as a Form of Obedience to God

Another important motivation for Christians to forgive is related to but different from the need to be forgiven by God. As was noted earlier, Christians particularly need to forgive because they have been forgiven. This is paramount as God is the ultimate forgiver of sins. This does not mean that Christians refuse to forgive their offenders and instead claim that only Jesus or God can forgive sins. God can forgive sins. This is why even Jesus asked his Father in heaven to forgive those who had offended him by falsely accusing him of blasphemy and subsequently crucifying him. This does not in any way change the fact that Jesus, while here on earth, repeatedly told people that their sins had been forgiven.

The woman caught in the act of adultery is a notable example in this regard. After the crowd had frog-marched the woman to where Jesus was, they accused the woman of adultery and went ahead to cite the Law of Moses, which expressly proved that such adulterers be stoned to death. To their utter amazement, Jesus, as the embodiment of the new dispensation of grace, had other ideas. Instead of condemning the woman with them, he demanded to know which among the accusers had never sinned so that he or she could be the one to throw the first stone at the woman. Since all had sinned, no one came forward. Instead, they started leaving one by one in total embarrassment. It could be argued that the real reason why all of them left is that Jesus accused them of refusing to forgive the woman as Jesus had taught them so many times.

The underlying message is that people find it easier to use excuses to not forgive than to forgive. In this regard, Jesus was a major stumbling block, especially to the traditional Jewish practices. Jesus was denying people the right to do what Moses had commanded, yet Jesus also made it clear that he had not come to abolish the law but fulfill it. Even to the most educated and learned legal scholars of that time, this also seemed like a contradiction, but it never was. Jesus indeed came to fulfill the Law because the law and the prophets always pointed to Jesus. When Jesus came into the world, he was the fulfillment of the Law, and as such, there was no need for the Law anymore. That is why he opposed certain practices supposedly demanded or allowed under the Law. Stoning adulterers to death as opposed to forgiving them and letting them go away scot-free was one of the changes Jesus introduced.

Jesus never did anything unless his Father explicitly authorized or demanded it of him. This means that Jesus never used his authority but the authority of God. Jesus was here on earth on what could be termed *delegated authority*. That is why he never claimed equality with God, even though he was God in all aspects. Therefore, Jesus, in forgiving sins, did not use his authority but the authority given him from the Father. This has far-reaching implications for Christians, especially when it comes to forgiving. One of them is that forgiving other people when they offend is based on delegated authority from God. This means that no one ought to withhold forgiveness on the pretext or excuse that only God can forgive sins. Instead, everyone is expected to forgive as a command from God who just as Jesus forgave in obedience to his heavenly Father. Jesus never shied away from forgiving people for their sins because the authority to forgive was with his heavenly Father.

Similarly, no Christians ought to shy away from forgiving based on the pretext that only God can forgive. Instead, all Christians should be motivated to forgive because God specifically demands that they forgive as they have been forgiven. It is a command from God that has to be obeyed without question and without considering the prevailing conditions. This is part of the reason why forgiving is hard—people see it as a command, and being a command from God, it requires to be done right. Christians, in particular, are concerned about not just doing what is right but also doing it right. Therefore, they tend to postpone forgiving or even not do it at all unless they are convinced they are doing it in the right way. Unfortunately, the many misconceptions that even Christians have about forgiveness mean it is hard to know when it is "right" to forgive and whether forgiving has been done in the right manner. In the end, they do not forgive at all, or they think they have forgiven when, in fact, they have not.

God demands that Christians forgive their brothers as they have been forgiven. He does not ask them to forgive if they feel like doing it or not to forgive if it is inconvenient for them to forgive. Therefore, Christians have to understand that forgiving the other person is a command, just like God forgives when people offend him and others. It does not matter how difficult it is or even how easy it is for people to hold onto unforgiveness. To humor God, just as Jesus honored God, Christians have to be willing and ready to forgive at all times and in all seasons. It is not a matter of choice or convenience; it is about obeying God. God specifically says that he is pleased with those who obey his commands. This means that he is much displeased with, even angry at, those who refuse to obey his commands. God readily punishes those who fail to obey his commands.

Being a command from God, forgiveness attracts specific punishment for violations just as there are specific punishments for violations of other commands. Jesus, answering Peter's question about how many times one ought to be forgiven, provided the number of times forgiveness ought to be grated and went ahead to specify the reward and penalty for not forgiving and forgiving (respectively):

> If you forgive men their trespasses, your heavenly Father will also forgive you. But if you do not forgive men their trespasses, neither will your Father forgive your trespasses.[103]

Therefore, not forgiving attracts a penalty just as forgiving attracts a reward from God. Most of the time, God is not concerned about the punishment for not forgiving—at least not as much as he is concerned about and interested in the rewards for forgiving. God is no unjust and is not keen on punishing his people. Instead, he wants them to be more like him and to hate evil. Since unforgiveness has many adverse outcomes, God does not like it and is inclined to discourage his people from refusing to forgive. However, the hardened hearts of human beings mean that they are naturally inclined toward doing evil. This is why punishment is prescribed for disobedience, including the refusal to forgive.

It is also essential to add that when God demanded believers to forgive those who sinned against them, he did not expect them to do it out of their power or might. Instead, he expected them to rely on the power of God. By their nature, human beings are limited in terms of what they can do out of their control. Human beings can do virtually nothing without the power

---

[103] Matthew 6:15 NIV.

of God. This is one of the reasons why forgiving is difficult for so many people, including Christians. It is not easy to tap into the power of God to forgive. If anything, few people know how to do this regularly or how to walk in the power of the Holy Spirit. As a result, many people attempt to forgive their offenders by using their understanding and knowledge. This is why they are doomed to fail even before they begin. The Bible teaches that in all situations, people ought to trust God and not lean on their own understanding.

The problem of people trying to lean on their understanding is that they do things outside the will of God or attempt to do something they cannot manage. The result is that God frustrates their efforts—or they fail to accomplish whatever they try to do using their power. Virtually every Christian readily admits that forgiving is one of the hardest things anyone can attempt to do. However, few of them will realize that they try to forgive based on their power and understanding as opposed to relying on the power of God. Some will even claim to always rely on the power of God, yet they will not be sure if they are filled with the Holy Ghost. Without the guidance and control of God through the Holy Spirit of God, forgiveness is bound to be difficult—or even impossible.

Jesus never tried to rely on his power when doing anything (even though he had immense power). That is why Jesus never attempted to free himself from those who persecuted and crucified Him on the cross. Instead, he submitted to the will of God who had sent him here on earth. Here was a mighty figure who was in all respects God but who chose not to rely on his power but the power of God. In forgiving people, Jesus always spoke of his Father in heaven and not himself:

> If you forgive men their trespasses, your heavenly Father will also forgive you. But if you do not forgive men their trespasses, neither will your Father forgive your trespasses."[104]

Jesus never referred to himself but for God in heaven. In the same way, Christians need to claim and use the power of God to help them forgive

---

[104] Matthew 6:15 NIV.

those who offend them. This is the only way they can achieve this. It is like the branches of a tree that can only bear fruit as long as they remain attached to the tree. If they are cut off—as God cuts off branches that do not bear fruit—they are useless except to be burned in the fire. Therefore, for Christians, abiding in God is mandatory and an essential survival strategy. It is also the only way that they can ever hope to be able to forgive other people and receive forgiveness from God. This, in itself, ought to be enough motivation for Christians to forgive. They ought to know that forgiving is not just a command from God; it is also one that God will enable them to accomplish. After all, as Paul told the Philippians:

I can do all things through Christ who strengthens me.[105]

---

[105] Philippians 4:12–13 NIV.

# CHAPTER 4

# THE FREEDOM IN FORGIVENESS

Forgiveness has been described in different ways and by using different words and qualifiers (adjectives) by different people. It mostly comes down to the person whose view about forgiveness is sought and their past experiences with forgiving (or not being able to forgive). For a large number of people, forgiveness is something good and bad at the same time. It is considered useful in that once people forgive, they tend to get some inner peace of mind that is unrivaled.[106] This is the same kind of inner peace that the apostle Paul described:

> And the peace of God, which transcends all understanding,
> will guard your hearts and your minds in Christ Jesus.[107]

On the other hand, not forgiving is often associated with deep hurts and struggles in trying to deal with the hurt. It matters little what people think of forgiveness and its benefits. What truly matters is what the Bible teaches about forgiveness, especially in terms of the freedom that comes with it. This is why this chapter explores the freedom associated with—or derived from—forgiveness.

---

[106] John F. MacArthur, *The Freedom and Power of Forgiveness*, electronic ed. (Wheaton, IL: Crossway Books, 1998), 24.
[107] Philippians 4:7 NIV.

## The Blessedness of Forgiveness

Before actually understanding how blessed it is to forgive, it is vital to understand the problems associated with not forgiving. After all, there would be no motivation to forgive if the refusal to forgive was okay or if forgiving had no benefits (such as freedom). In this regard, it is essential to examine Paul's exhortation above to the Philippians critically. Why did he refer to a peace that transcends human understanding, and how could anyone possibly get such a peace? According to Paul, this peace that transcends human understanding comes to anyone who chooses not to be anxious about anything:

> Do not be anxious about anything, but in every situation, by prayer and petition, with thanksgiving, present your requests to God.[108]

Therefore, the message here is that lack of anxiety is the key to having a peace that transcends human understanding. Conversely, those who are anxious about anything will not have peace of mind, and their minds will be troubled.

This message by Paul to the Philippians is included here not necessarily because it addresses the issue of forgiveness directly but because it highlights one of the feelings or symptoms associated with unforgiveness. In this passage of scripture, the core message by the apostle is for the believers to learn not to be troubled by the issues and concerns of this world but always to learn to pray to God and make supplications to him. According to Paul, when people "pray and make supplications to God with thanksgiving," they can experience true peace of mind.

Remarkably, failure to forgive has consequences similar to those described by Paul. When people refuse to forgive for whatever reason, their hearts become greatly troubled. They always hurt, and as a result, they go about hurting other people near and around them. The pain of the hurt causes them to be in a perpetual state of bitterness and anger occasioned by the refusal to forgive and compounded by the damage caused by the offense. The pain and hurt make it hard (or even impossible) for them to

---

[108] Philippians 4:6 NIV.

even think about praying to God and seeking to be freed from the constant pain and hurting. The reality is that if such people were to only offer prayers and supplications to God together with thanksgiving, God would deliver them from this hurt and grant them peace of mind.

The problem is that people who have refused to forgive are not usually ready to pray. When they are Christians, they also understand that God will not hear their prayers unless they have forgiven. Therefore, people often choose not to pray because they know if they have to pray, then they have to forgive. Since they do not want to forgive in the first place, they also decide not to pray to God and commit their concerns and troubles to him. The result is that they keep hurting and endure the pain and suffering that comes with it. Paul addressed the Philippians:

Rejoice in the Lord always [and] Let [their] gentleness be evident to all [because] ... the Lord is near.[109]

Other than the loss of inner peace, another negative effect of refusal to forgive is the loss of inner joy. Naturally, God expects his people—especially those who are called by his name—always to be people given to anger and bitterness.

Whenever people refuse to forgive, the hurt occasioned by the offense (as well as the continuing pain caused by the continued refusal to let go of the offender) robs them of their inner joy.[110] The person may try to look healthy and okay from the outside—and even claim to be so—but in reality, they are profoundly hurting inside. Unfortunately, these deep hurts have the most effect on the soul of the individual, and unless they are addressed through forgiveness, the individual may become irritable, bitter, and prone to bouts of anger. The individual ends up hurting virtually every person aground them because they are so obsessed with revenge that they cannot afford to think objectively.[111]

It would be an injustice to talk about the blessedness that comes from

[109] Philippians 4:4–5 NIV.
[110] John F. MacArthur, *The Freedom and Power of Forgiveness*, electronic ed. (Wheaton, IL: Crossway Books, 1998), 26.
[111] F. LeRon Shults and Steven J. Sandage, *The Faces of Forgiveness: Searching for Wholeness and Salvation* (Grand Rapids, MI: Baker Academic, 2003), 43.

forgiveness without talking about what the Bible expressly says about this issue. Few other people capture the blessedness of forgiveness than the Palmist who said, "Blessed is he whose transgressions are forgiven, whose sins are covered."[112] When it comes to the blessedness associated with forgiveness, it matters little if the person is the one of forgiving or being forgiven. The one thing that seems to matter is that forgiveness has taken place, and a person no longer has to bear the heavy burden of unforgiveness together with its hurtful feelings of revenge and anger. As long as a person has received forgiveness or has forgiven, a blessedness only known to God comes about. Whatever such people do henceforth, the blessings of God flow freely and almost endlessly in their lives.

God is the one who forgives and covers people's sins and transgressions. This means that as long as sins are not forgiven or uncovered, God's blessings cannot flow in the lives of the people responsible for not forgiving. Such people mostly happen to be those who have refused to forgive those who have offended them. This is something that occurs so often that it has become almost standard practice for people not to forgive. They may talk about God's blessings and quote virtually every other verse in the Bible on blessedness, but they fail to realize that God cannot bless them because they have refused to forgive. Perhaps it is just more comfortable for people to claim and proclaim God's blessings over their lives. That could be why they do this fairly quickly and frequently. However, they fail to recognize and appreciate the fact that God operates based on firmly established principles.

One of these principles is that while he has decreed blessings over his people, these blessings are based on his people obeying God's Word. If believers do not obey God's Word, they cannot possibly expect to enjoy an abundance of blessings from God. This is not how God planned this to be. Because God is only bound by his Word and cannot be swayed or corrupted, he only acts if his Word is invoked. However, the same Word of God that promises to send blessings to his people also says that it is only the people whose sins are forgiven and transgressions covered who are blessed. This means that it is only in the context of forgiveness that God's blessings can flow. Therefore, forgiveness effectively opens and unleashes

---

[112] Psalm 32:1 NIV.

God's blessings to flow into the lives of the people who have chosen to be selfless by forgiving those who sin against them.

## Forgiveness as a Source of Freedom

Refusal to forgive is markedly similar to a hostage-taking situation where people are forcefully captured and detained without their consent. Hostage takers often demand ransom in exchange for the hostages. In essence, it is when the payment is paid that the hostages are released. After they are released, they mostly get back all their freedom, albeit with some awful memories of the situation. Forgiving is in many ways similar to freeing people from a hostage situation. It is the same as rescuing someone from a hostage situation. The only difference is that the person being saved is the same person who has made oneself a hostage. It may sound awful, even false, that anyone can willingly let themselves into a hostage situation (or allow themselves to be taken hostage). In a real hostage-taking case, no one readily accepts being taken hostage but only goes along when it becomes clear that there is no other way out of the situation. Those who refuse to be taken captive often risk death. There is usually no need to risk death when there is a possibility of being rescued or somehow coming out of the situation alive.

When people refuse to forgive one another, the tendency is to assume they have power over their offenders—and part of that power is used to detain them or hold them captive.[113] This is one of the greatest fallacies and ironies associated with unforgiveness. The reality is that offended people usually take themselves hostage when they refuse to forgive their offenders. Afterward, they hold themselves captive and experience all the problems that come with captivity, unaware that they can let themselves out if they choose.[114] They can want to free themselves from captivity by forgiving their offenders.

---

[113] Alistair McFadyen and Marcel Sarot, *Forgiveness and Truth* (Edinburgh, New York: T&T Clark, 2001), 27.

[114] John F. MacArthur, *The Freedom and Power of Forgiveness*, electronic ed. (Wheaton, IL: Crossway Books, 1998), 29.

Therefore, forgiveness is a source of freedom like no other.[115] This freedom is different and unique because it is the freedom of the offended person and not that of the offender. Offenders do get some measure of liberty resulting from forgiveness, but this is nowhere close to the level of freedom the offended person receives. The offender certainly gets certain benefits, such as previously withheld love, kindness, gentleness, and even joy and patience. These seem to be the same things that Paul spoke of:

> But the fruit of the Spirit is love, joy, peace, patience, kindness, goodness, faithfulness, gentleness, self-control, against such things, there is no law. If we live by the Spirit, let us also walk by the Spirit.[116]

Typically, refusing to forgive leads people to withhold certain things from the offender, and in doing so, they feel that they have control and power over them. This sense of power and control is false in that it is usually just a way of concealing the offended person's vulnerabilities and hurts. Still, the most critical issue is that forgiveness results in the offended person finally being able to release whatever they were withholding from the offender. Depending on the offense, many offended people withhold many things from their offenders as a way of paying them back. Therefore, forgiving releases these things to be enjoyed by the offender while these things are mostly in the form of emotions; being released to the offender results in immense freedom for both parties. The offended person is finally free of the burden of having to withhold good things, such as goodness, love, care, mercy, friendship, and other benefits due to the offender. Most importantly, the offended person is finally free from having to bear the pain and suffering associated with having to live with many bottled-up negative emotions, such as rage, anger, bitterness, and vengeance.

These are the natural feelings that offended people harbor toward their offenders. The longer the person refuses to forgive, the more substantial this burden usually becomes until it reaches a point when it can no longer be borne. At that time, the offended person has only two choices: to forgive

[115] Derek Prince, *The Three Most Powerful Words: Discovering the Freedom of Releasing the Ones Who Hurt Us* (Charlotte, NC: Derek Prince Ministries, 2006), 35.
[116] Galatians 5:22–25 NIV.

or waste away from the bottled-up anger and resentment. Those who choose not to forgive often end up suffering from more serious emotional, psychological, and even physical conditions.

Forgiving releases the anger and resentment and frees the person just as one would feel after being let out of a hostage-taking situation or prison for the first time after a long time.[117] In essence, this kind of freedom comes from being set free from the deeds of the flesh. These deeds of the flesh, according to Paul, include:

> Enmities, strife, jealousy, outbursts of anger, disputes, dissensions, factions, envying … and things like these, of which I forewarn you … that those who practice such things shall not inherit the kingdom of God."[118]

From the Bible, refusal to forgive, which is akin to having an unforgiving spirit, effectively prevents the offended person from being able to walk in the Spirit as is required of every believer. According to Paul, when people walk in the Spirit, they cannot gratify the works of the flesh:

> This I say then, "Walk in the Spirit, and ye shall not fulfill the lust of the flesh."[119]

Therefore, walking in the Spirit, which is only possible if someone has forgiven or if someone has a forgiving spirit, allows the person the freedom to be in constant communion with God. Most importantly, walking in the Spirit prevents someone from being able to gratify the desires of the flesh. It is indeed a form of slavery when a person cannot do as they please because of sin.

Paul said that when people do not walk in the Spirit, they will gratify the desires of their flesh, and as a result, they will not be able to do the desires of the Spirit. This means they are slaves to their evil desires. It is discomforting enough just having to think of a situation where one's own

---

[117] Alistair McFadyen and Marcel Sarot, *Forgiveness and Truth* (Edinburgh, New York: T&T Clark, 2001), 9.

[118] Galatians 5:19–21 NIV.

[119] Galatians 5:16 KJV.

sinful desires enslave a person. The person may want to do what is right and acceptable—such as loving their neighbor as they love themselves or leading a righteous life—but they cannot because they are prevented from doing so by their unforgiving spirits. Paul also describes this situation:

God cannot be mocked. Everyone reaps what they sow.[120]

As long as people insist on not forgiving, they are effectively sowing the seeds of discord, anger, envy, hatred, and other negative emotions. As a result of that, they have to be ready to reap the fruits of these seeds because everyone reaps what they sow.

In reality, the fruits of the flesh are not what anyone should ever look forward to producing. Refusing to forgive sets up a person for a life of trouble and of doing what is socially unacceptable. The person gets overly consumed with the desire to do what is wrong or evil. Therefore, it ought not to come as a surprise that there are people who always seem bent on doing what is harmful both to themselves and others. They are still angry, malicious, jealous, envious, and hateful. The list of the evil deed they commit is almost endless. However, most people rarely stop to imagine that all these evil deeds could be the result of unforgiveness. Most of the time, it is believed that the person is just evil by choice. While it is true that the person may decide to forgive by choice, their evil deeds are hardly ever of their choosing. Instead, the evil deeds are merely fruits of not agreeing to walk in the Spirit and instead preferring to walk in the flesh owing to their unforgiveness.

If the person could be honest, they would admit to making every effort possible not to live a sinful life and failing in every attempt. The reason they fail is that they are by default designed to be evil and bear the fruits of the flesh as opposed to those of the Spirit. Therefore, their problem lies not in seeking ways to stop being evil but in letting go of their anger, resentment, and hatred by forgiving those who have offended them. Once they forgive, the stage is set for them to start living a life of freedom—freedom from having to gratify the desires of the sinful nature. This happens because those who choose to forgive are freed from this law

---

[120] Galatians 6:7–8 NIV.

of life and death that prevents people from doing whatever they desire to do. By choosing to forgive, they can start walking in the Spirit once again, and in doing so, they can no longer gratify the evil desires of the flesh. Instead, they bear the fruits of the Spirit. Therefore, forgiveness is a source of immense freedom.

It is no wonder that it is so difficult to forgive. One cannot possibly imagine having to continually live a sinful life as a result of merely refusing to forgive someone for an offense that could be minor compared to the offenses the offender person ends up committing against others. If forgiveness were more natural to accomplish, few people would ever have to walk in the flesh due to unforgiveness. Instead, they would be eager to forgive and walk in the Spirit. Therefore, it can be argued that one of the reasons why forgiveness is hard is because Satan is bent on ensuring that God's people do not forgive. Satan knows that as long as the people of God remain in a state of unforgiveness, God will not be pleased with them and will move through the Holy Spirit to convict them. Without the ability to walk in the Spirit, these people will have to walk in the flesh and gratify the desires of the flesh. This is what Satan ultimately wants.

It is not that Satan cannot use other techniques to prevent God's people from walking in the Spirit. There are many alternatives and options available to him. However, he elects to use some of the seemingly less serious issues of life. There is no denying that many Christians do not even think—let alone believe—that unforgiveness is sin and that it can result in consequences similar to those caused by seemingly serious or "bigger" sins like murder, fornication, and adultery. The reality is that, before God, all sins are equal and attract the same punishment.

The only sin that seems to have some special recognition and seems to be different in that respect is the sin of grieving the Holy Spirit. In this regard, God says there is no forgiveness for such a sin:

> He that is not with me is against me, and he that gathereth not with me scattereth abroad. Wherefore I say unto you, all manner of sin and blasphemy shall be forgiven unto men: but the blasphemy against the Holy Ghost shall not be forgiven unto men. And whosoever speaketh a word against the Son of man, it shall be forgiven him:

but whosoever speaketh against the Holy Ghost, it shall not be forgiven him, neither in this world, neither in the world to come.[121]

On the specific subject of not grieving the Holy Spirit, it is also written that:

And grieve not the Holy Spirit of God, whereby ye are sealed unto the day of redemption. Let all bitterness, and wrath, and anger, and clamor, and evil speaking, be put away from you, with all malice: And be ye kind one to another, tenderhearted, forgiving one another, even as God for Christ's sake hath forgiven you.[122]

God takes a personal interest in the sin of grieving the Holy Spirit. Those who grieve the Holy Spirit may not be forgiven by God as there is no grace left after that. The Bible does not explain the meaning of grieving the Holy Spirit. However, the Holy Spirit is grieved when he is not allowed to do as he is supposed to do or when his work is hindered by sin. This mostly happens when the person walks in the flesh and gratifies the desires of the flesh. Without the help of the Holy Spirit, people cannot accomplish much.

## Freedom of Forgiving Oneself

Forgiveness is complicated and sometimes problematic, partly because many people are hesitant to forgive themselves or admit that whatever they have done deserves to be forgiven or can be forgiven. As bizarre as this may sound, it represents the reality for many people and is, therefore, one of the significant reasons why forgiveness is exhausting. In practice, as is in theory, forgiveness is only possible in a context where the people affected by an offense are ready to forgive. This includes forgiving the other person and forgiving oneself where need be. Today, one of the significant challenges that pastors across the world, including those in this country,

---

[121] Matthew 12:30–32 KJV.
[122] Ephesians 4:30–32 KJV.

is not just the refusal by people to forgive others but also their refusal to forgive themselves. For some unexplained reasons, many people prefer to be hard on themselves and to reject any ideas that imply that whatever they have done can be forgiven or is "forgivable."

There is still controversy even among theologians and Bible scholars regarding whether God forgives all sins or whether some sins are unforgivable. However, the Bible makes it clear that God forgives all sins except the sin of grieving the Holy Spirit. As was noted before, all sins that people commit against other people are forgivable. There is no question whatsoever about that. However, the sin committed against the Holy Spirit is not forgivable—not even by God. This means that when people grieve the Holy Spirit or sin against the Holy Spirit, they cannot expect to be forgiven for such sins. Jesus made that clear:

> Wherefore I say unto you, All manner of sin and blasphemy shall be forgiven unto men: but the blasphemy against the Holy Ghost shall not be forgiven unto men. And whosoever speaketh a word against the Son of man, it shall be forgiven him: but whosoever speaketh against the Holy Ghost, it shall not be forgiven him, neither in this world, neither in the world to come.[123]

This passage of scripture indicates that blasphemy against the Holy Spirit and speaking against the Holy Spirit are the two sins that cannot be forgiven. In this regard, it matters not whether a person repents of one's sins. Such sins are not forgivable and cannot be forgiven.

This could explain why Paul made it clear that he was not talking about the so-called unpardonable sin (grieving the Holy Spirit). Subsequently, there is no reason why anyone would think or imagine that their offense or sin cannot be forgiven. Even worse is the thought or assumption that certain offenses are not forgivable. The reality is that such deception comes from the evil one who would like to see Christians suffering under the burden and yoke of unforgiveness. Satan takes great pride and pleasure

---

[123] Matthew 12:31–32 KJV.

in keeping God's people captive in different ways, and ensuring that they do not forgive themselves—and others—is one of the strategies he uses.

God is perfectly able to forgive all sins and is more than willing to forgive. However, some people decide that their sins are not forgivable or that God would be unwilling to forgive their sins because, in their belief, their sins are too severe to be forgiven. God approaches the issue of forgiveness differently. The Bible is explicitly clear that Jesus died on the cross for the remission of the sins of the world. It does not make any attempt to separate sin into categories; it refers to them as a whole. This means that it is false for anyone to believe or claim that God cannot forgive certain sins they have committed.

It is essential to add at this point that the two sins, as mentioned earlier, that are not pardonable or forgivable have nothing to do with humans sinning against other humans. Most of the time, the sins that people need to be forgiven for and to forgive are those that involve offenses against other people. They are not sins against the Holy Spirit. Even if they were sins against the Holy Spirit, Jesus made it clear that only two sins against the Holy Spirit are not forgivable. These are blaspheming the Holy Spirit and speaking against the Holy Spirit. It is, therefore, possible that even certain sins against the Holy Spirit could be forgivable. The bottom line is that only two specific sins are not excusable, and these two are not easy for anyone to commit. On the contrary, virtually all the other sins—and the ones that people commit regularly—are forgivable.

Because of refusing to forgive themselves, many people also find it hard to forgive others. The same reasoning seems to become dominant when it comes to sinning against other people. This is why it was noted at the start of this section that forgiveness is only possible within a context where the people affected by offense are willing and ready to forgive. If one or more of the people affected are not willing to forgive for any reason, forgiveness is bound to be difficult—or even impossible. When people cannot forgive themselves for committing a particular sin and are instead bitter and overly concerned about the sin, they will more often than not refuse to forgive other people when they offend them. Such people will think that the person who has hurt them has committed too grave a sin to be forgiven. As has been noted earlier, the same kind of reasoning that stops or prevents the person from forgiving oneself will also prevent them from forgiving other people. Most of the time, such people happen to be more interested in the so-called magnitude of an offense than doing what is right or acceptable before God.

For some reason, such people will rate sins based on their perceived magnitude and choose to forgive or not forgive based on the perceived size of the sin. Therefore, they will readily forgive if they consider the offense to be minor but refuse to forgive when they feel the sin is significant. There is no telling how they arrive at such scales given the fact that before God, all sins are equal. Such people may have many preconceived misconceptions about sin and refuse to consider any other possibility. Once again, this emphasizes the argument that the many mistakes that people have of and about forgiveness (and by extension about sin) contribute significantly to making it hard to forgive. If people understood that all sin is equal in the sight of God and that God punishes all sin equally just as he forgives sin, then there is reason to believe that they would be more willing and ready to forgive. This is because they will not be as hard on themselves when they sin as usually happens every so often with their so-called major or big sins.

Realizing that all sins are equal, people are more likely to be able to forgive themselves and, by extension, forgive others. It all comes down to realizing that before God, there is no such thing as an awful sin or thing. Therefore, people ought not to think that they have done something so terrible or out of place that God cannot forgive them. Human beings may refuse to forgive other rational people for sins or offenses they consider to be awful. However, God always forgives even such sins. Since God has the ultimate say when it comes to forgiving, it matters less whether an offense is forgiven by fellow people as it does whether God forgives the person.

It is essential for people to seek forgiveness from other people and forgive them as well. However, it is also possible for some people to decline to forgive their offense even when forgiveness is sought. In such cases, the offending people ought not to be overly hard on themselves and think that God is not happy with them or that he cannot forgive their sins. Just because other people refuse to forgive an offender does not mean that God will also follow suit and withhold forgiveness. God is sovereign and is not bound by anything except his Word. Since his Word says that he is a God of mercy and will readily forgive sin, people should expect him to do just that: forgive their sins.

It is in understanding that God is merciful and ready and willing to forgive all kinds of sin that freedom to the offense comes into play. As long as people fail to forgive themselves, a lot of liberty is forfeited. They remain in bondage and cannot free themselves from it for as long as the negative thoughts are held onto and not released. Usually, the problem is not that the people concerned are inherently wrong or evil. In many cases where there is a refusal to forgive both oneself and others, the people concerned are people of high standing in society. They have been brought up and raised in God-fearing families and have godly parents. They are also people who have been raised in the church and who are supposed to have a better understanding of the teachings of the Bible. They are also not children; most are adults who may have spent much of their time serving in ministry or even leading other congregants. Yet they are faced with the tragedy of refusing to forgive themselves and others. The problem is that they have to fully grasp and understand the meaning of forgiveness.

As a result, God's intended purpose for the lives of such people is hardly ever realized because they live in self-imposed bondage. They are often not willing to explore the possibility of forgiving themselves and others just as God has forgiven them. Instead, they usually have a form of self-righteousness that is more a reflection of religion than faith. Being religious does not necessarily mean that a person has faith. In this regard, it can be argued that Christ never taught people to belong to religions but to become believers in the message of the cross. Therefore, God is not interested in religion or religious practices. He is moved by obedience to his Word. Like the Pharisees, self-righteous people often find themselves trapped in self-imposed bondage. They think they know everything or that they are better than everyone else by being firm and strict in their observance of religious rules and practices. They believe that they know more than everyone else, including understanding more about sin and forgiveness than anyone else.

As a result, these people have prevented themselves from opening their hearts to God and letting the Holy Spirit teach and guide them in the way of righteousness. Unfortunately, this is not the attitude that God desires for his people. Instead of God infilling them with his Holy Spirit, he has allowed them to pursue their selfish ambitions and follow their depraved minds to whatever leads them. In the end, they never grasp the full immensity of the forgiveness of God. This bondage stifles their capacity to love and accept those who they know deserve their love.

For those who are married, unforgiveness keeps them in the bondage of crippled marriages. Such marriages may start on the wrong footing and remain so for a long time. Unfortunately, such slavery occasioned by unforgiveness runs through generations and gets passed on from one generation to another. This is why such people hardly ever, if at all, bear much fruit even though they claim to be Christians. This happens because the evil root of unforgiveness chokes out the otherwise abundant life that Christ so graciously promised and pours out to those who daily depend on him and seek the guidance of the Holy Spirit.

People in bondage who fail to forgive themselves or others tend to be extremely hostile to others. Even though most people hardly recognize or become aware of it, hostility from one relationship almost always negatively affects the ability of a person to get along with other people. This often manifests when hurting people attempt to work out their differences with other people and fail. In fact, the more people try to do this, the less likely it becomes for them to succeed. The real reason why they fail is that they are hurting from a different relationship. Therefore, they tend to carry the hurt to other relationships; in doing so, they end up hurting other people. Yet they think that the other people are the problem.

When people choose to forgive, one of the greatest freedoms that comes their way is not being able to hurt others. It is frustrating enough for people to try to establish new relationships and form new friendships with other people and fail because of not having forgiven. Instead, they carry the pain and hurt to every other relationship. People want to be loved and accepted, and when they cannot successfully establish new relationships, they feel like it is rejection toward them as opposed to what they have refused not to forgive. Such people will usually come up with different excuses to conceal the underlying problem. As soon as they become tired of trying to resolve their differences with other people, they become inclined to excuse their lack of sensitivity. They may even claim that being insensitive is part of their personality and that they cannot do anything to change it. Subsequently, they develop the annoying attitude of expecting other people to accept them as they are. This is when they start hurting other people without even realizing it.

Forgiving helps people stop hurting themselves and other people. It may not be so much of an issue when other people are injured. After all, it could be said to be their business and that they could find their ways of avoiding the hurt. However, it is bondage for a person to be hurting. Such pain can only be overcome by forgiving. It does not matter who was to blame for the offense or how legitimate the affected person's complaint is against the offender. The one thing that ultimately matters is that only forgiving helps alleviate the hurting. Therefore, forgiving is an antidote for deep hurts inflicted or caused by other people.

## Freedom from God's Punishment

It is good enough for people to be freed from the hurting experienced as a result of not being able to forgive or refusing to forgive. However, many other freedoms can come about as a result of forgiving. One of them is that one gets acceptance from God and is, therefore, freed from God's punishment. This is one of the issues that are least talked about, but that is most important when it comes to forgiveness. It is true that the effect of the hurting caused by unforgiveness is a major one and undoubtedly the one with the most far-reaching implications. However, unforgiveness is also associated with God's wrath. After all, God is not pleased when people do not forgive because unforgiveness in the strictest sense is a form of wrongdoing and is, therefore, sin in itself. Since all wrongdoing is sin, it follows that unforgiveness is sin and will subsequently attract the full penalty prescribed for sin.

The Bible makes it clear that no sin will go unpunished by God. In his letter to the Church at Galatia, Paul said, "Do not be deceived; God is not mocked; for whatever a man sows, this he will also reap."[124] This could not be further from the truth. Every sin meets its full punishment, and understanding this is a good starting point in appreciating the importance and freedom of forgiveness. Understanding that sin attracts penalty and that unforgiveness is a sin should lead people to know that one of the outcomes associated with forgiving is being able to be freed from the risk of being punished by God. This has nothing to do with the offender but the

---

[124] Galatians 6:7 NIV.

offended person. It is for the offended person to choose to forgive or risk being punished by God for disobedience or sinning by refusing to forgive.

This implies that offended people may suffer double jeopardy if they fail to forgive by use in addition to the hurt they experience; they also risk suffering from the punishment prescribed by God. If people were wise enough, they would forgive to avoid the second consequence of having to face God's punishment. Yet God's discipline is not always the best punishment there can ever be. Some people would prefer to fall in the hands of God than the hands of men because God is gracious while men are evil. However, God's grace does not necessarily mean that his wrath cannot be rekindled when people go on sinning without any restraint.

The more sin increases, the more grace abounds. However, people ought not to sin so that grace may abound even more. It is like the prophecy that the Son of Man would come into the world and suffer even unto death at the hands of evil men. However, the men who persecuted and betrayed Jesus were still held accountable for their actions. This may seem unfair on the part of God because Christ was destined to be betrayed and persecuted anyway. Yet God still ensured that despite the prophecy, those who took part in the evil deeds of killing the Messiah were punished for their sin. Among other issues, this could be an indication of how seriously God takes the problem of sin. Therefore, unforgiveness is sin and is punishable just like every other sin; this shows how seriously God regards the issue of forgiveness.

God also makes the solemn promise to the Israelites that he "will not acquit the guilty."[125] Moreover, it is written that "The Lord will by no means leave the guilty unpunished"[126] and that "God's wrath is revealed … against all ungodliness and unrighteousness."[127] These and other commands or promises indicate that God is not partial even though he is merciful. On the one hand, he sent his only begotten Son to die on the cross for the remission of sin and, in doing so, effectively freed humanity from the need to be punished for their sins. On the other hand, he still holds to account everyone who repeatedly sins on purpose. This is because

---

[125] Exodus 23:7 NIV.
[126] Nahum 1:3 NIV.
[127] Romans 1:1 NIV.

ROBERT E. GAINES SR., PHD

there is no more blood left for the remission of sin if people continue to sin after they have been graciously forgiven. Every person had sinned and fallen short of the glory of God. Therefore, everyone was due to receive their just punishment from God. However, God took away the sins of the entire world not because anyone deserved to be forgiven but out of the grace of the Lord Jesus Christ.

Sometimes people falsely think that by God being gracious—or this being the dispensation of grace—God will remove the consequences of their sins. God forgives sin, but he does not do so by simply turning away his head and looking the other way when people sin. Instead, he is much grieved whenever people—especially believers—sin. That is why he will readily punish all sin committed. If God's people sin, they are at a state of enmity with God. Admittedly, it is better to forgive than to be in a constant state of hostility with God because people always seek the downfall of their enemies. There is nothing good that an enemy can ever do for someone they consider to be the enemy.

Therefore, forgiveness results in freedom in that the forgiver effectively makes the transition from being an enemy of God by having sinned (by not forgiving) to being a friend of God. When people's enemies become their friends, many people heave a sigh of relief since they no longer must be on constant watch for what the person is up to after becoming friends. The distrust that usually exists between enemies ceases when they become friends. Rather than expecting evil from the enemy, one can now expect good. The same happens between God and the people who choose to forgive their offenders. God relents in his anger and embraces the person. After all, there is great rejoicing in heaven when people turn away from their evil ways and start doing what is right.

Just as God promises to deal firmly with sin by punishing all those who sin, he also promises that no sin is beyond forgiving. It is also written that even the ungodly get justification from God.[128] This should be a significant motivation to forgive as it is one of the greatest freedoms that one can ever get from forgiving. As a result of forgiving, everyone could expect to be forgiven just as even the vilest sinner can expect to receive the

---

[128] Romans 4:5 NIV.

saving grace of Jesus Christ. In describing to the Romans, the blessedness that comes with forgiveness of sins, Paul said:

> Even as David also describeth the blessedness of the man, unto whom God imputeth righteousness without works, Saying, Blessed are they whose iniquities are forgiven, and whose sins are covered. Blessed is the man to whom the Lord will not impute sin. Cometh this blessedness then upon the circumcision only, or upon the uncircumcision also? for we say that faith was reckoned to Abraham for righteousness.[129]

When it comes to God forgiving sin, there is no partiality. It does not matter whether a person is a believer (circumcised) or a nonbeliever (uncircumcised). The most important consideration is that sin is forgiven—and transgressions are covered. Once this condition or principle is met, God's blessings follow in an unrestricted manner. This is arguably the positive side of the whole issue of forgiveness. The negative side is that refusal to forgive results in punishment because unforgiveness is sin. The positive side is that God does relent in his anger and often forgives and covers the sins of people. While some sins may not be forgiven even by God, all sins can be covered. Therefore, people who forgive can rest assured that they are eligible to receive justification from God—at least as far as the aspect of unforgiveness is concerned. People get justified when their sins are forgiven. Similarly, forgiving—and by extension, letting go of the sin of unforgiveness—should also result in justification.

---

[129] Romans 4:6–9 KJV.

# CHAPTER 5

# THE PROCESS OF FORGIVENESS

Contrary to the notion that forgiveness is instantaneous, it takes a process. Most importantly, it is when the process of forgiveness is followed to the end that true forgiveness can result. Otherwise, there is a risk that forgiveness will not happen as a result of one or more steps or processes not being followed or having been overlooked. As would be expected, the Bible does not have any specific formula to be followed by people who have been hurt when they are seeking to forgive. Instead, different passages of scripture address various issues about forgiveness in different contexts. Therefore, different approaches to the process of forgiveness have come up.

This chapter presents and discusses one of the several possible processes that can be used to achieve forgiveness. The different methods available have similarities and differences with the one shown in this chapter. Mostly, the differences are only in the choice of words or in the order in which specific activities have to be undertaken.

## Forgiveness as a Process

Understanding the process of forgiveness has to be commensurate with understanding and acknowledging that forgiveness is indeed a process and not an event.[130] There may be some aspects of forgiveness that make it an event. An example is when an offender comes to the offended person

---

[130] Derek Prince, *The Three Most Powerful Words: Discovering the Freedom of Releasing the Ones Who Hurt Us* (Charlotte, NC: Derek Prince Ministries, 2006), 13.

and asks to be forgiven. If the offended person agrees to and forgives the offender, then the forgiveness is in that regard an event because it has happened momentarily. However, this is usually not how forgiveness happens. Even if an offender personally goes to the offended person and asks to be forgiven (and is forgiven), there is more that the forgiving person needs to do afterward. This means that forgiveness can only seem like an event, but in reality, it is a process. Even when it is regarded as an event, this can only be from the offender and not the offended person because only the offender can be forgiven instantaneously. After all, there is nothing extra that the offender needs (such as healing from the hurt). On the other hand, the offended person has to heal from the damage after the forgiveness, and since healing takes time, forgiveness becomes a process and not an event.

Indeed, it can be argued that the word "forgiveness" contains the word "gift," which could mean that choosing to forgive the offended person mainly offers a gift to the offender. While this is debatable, pardoning indeed entails or includes gifting someone the freedom from needing to pay the cost or penalty of having caused pain and hurt to the offended person. Still, this view can only hold if the offender shares the same opinion, which is not always the case. In fact, there are times when the offender thinks that the offense was justified and that forgiving is not a gift at all (or if it is a gift, then it is a gift to the offended person). Without regard to the different views on the culpability of the offender and the offended person in an offense, it cannot be denied that forgiving entails the offended people releasing the offender from the responsibility or expectation of having to pay for the harm caused to them. Therefore, forgiving could indeed be regarded as a gift to the offender in this regard.

The problem is usually that the kind of gift inherent in forgiveness is never easy to give. On the contrary, it is one of the hardest gifts anyone can ever be asked to provide. While other gifts require just a moment to give to the recipient, the reward associated with forgiveness often requires a long, drawn-out process to give to the rightful recipient. This could be an indication that forgiveness is one of the most valuable gifts ever since it is only the precious and useful things that people find hard to give away. If forgiveness were cheap and easy to get, giving it would not have been as difficult as it has proven to be.

The good thing with the gift of forgiveness—and one that ought to be a motivation even for offended people—is that as it is given, the giver also gets part of the gift. This is usually in the form of the hate-free and grudge-free life the offended person gets to live after that. This life of total freedom from the burden of bearing drudges and resentments against the offender is only possible after one has forgiven from the heart. It is little wonder, therefore, that Moses commanded the Israelites and said, "Do not seek revenge or bear a grudge against one of your people, but love your neighbor as yourself."[131] Instead of revenge, it is important to forgive.

## Offense, Rebuke, Forgiveness

Luke's account of forgiving seems to point to the need for the physical meeting between the offender and the offended person as part of the process of forgiving or for forgiveness to occur. Luke records Jesus commanding his disciples:

> If your brother sins, rebuke him, and if he repents, forgive him. If he sins against you seven times in a day, and seven times comes back to you and says, "I repent," forgive him.[132]

This passage is an illustration of why forgiveness is one of the most challenging things to do for many human beings. It matters little whether a person is born again or not. All people struggle to forgive, and these two short verses contain most of the reasons why it is hard to forgive. Therefore, it is essential to analyze these two verses critically.

The other important aspect concerning this passage of scripture is that it makes two of the most critical, yet difficult commands ever made by Jesus. The first one is to rebuke, and the second one is to forgive. In a way, Jesus was trying to give his disciples a quick approach to the process of forgiving, and issues to do with the process of forgiving are dealt with in a different chapter. The vital point in this chapter concerns the misconceptions about forgiveness. Jesus demands that when it comes to an

---

[131] Leviticus 19:18 NIV.
[132] Luke 17:3–4 NIV.

offense between two people, the offended person has two obligations: to rebuke the offender and forgive the offender. Reprimanding an offended person may seem easy, but it is challenging if one understands what it truly means.

To "rebuke" as used in this context means to be able to rebuke someone in a tentative manner, which effectively means prosecuting a case against the offender with a lot of caution. It does not mean being able to pursue a claim against the offender in such a way that the offender is convicted of the crime, which he has been accused of without the proper evidence. Even though this second meaning of the term "rebuke" is also used in the New Testament, the context provided in the preceding verse in Luke does not refer to this meaning. Instead, it refers to the first meaning where caution and tentativeness are required in the prosecution of the case against the person. Either way, rebuking an offender is never an easy task because it is human nature for the offended person not to want to be under any obligation for an offense he or she did not commit the first place. Instead, it seems only right that all the commitments be given to the offender.[133]

This means that even requiring the offended person to go to the offender is hard enough and an issue of great concern for people. The reasoning on the part of the offender is about why they ought to take the first step when they had no role in the offense and especially when the offender did not even show any remorse over or concern for the offense and instead acted as though nothing happened. Still, Jesus commands that the offended person goes to the offender and rebukes them. At least from Jesus, it matters little, if at all, who goes to the other first. The one issue that ultimately matters is for a rebuke to be made to the offender by the offended person.

Perhaps if such rebuke could reach the offender differently, then Jesus would have relieved the offended person from the obligation to go to the offender. However, there is no way a rebuke could reach the offender in the way Jesus designed it to be made without the offender physically meeting with the offended person. Moreover, and this is the most important part, Jesus must have understood that in the end, it is the offended person and

---

[133] Derek Prince, *The Three Most Powerful Words: Discovering the Freedom of Releasing the Ones Who Hurt Us* (Charlotte, NC: Derek Prince Ministries, 2006), 45.

not the offender who will benefit from the rebuke—and the subsequent forgiveness. Therefore, he must have reasoned that the offended person needed to be the one to seek out the offender. Therefore, offended people have to find the courage to take the right step as commanded by Jesus: find the offender. This requirement serves to underscore just how difficult forgiving is.

In this regard, the precursor to forgiving—rebuking the offender—seems to be so much challenging, stressful, and overwhelming to the offended people, and as a result, many people do not even attempt to find the offender—let alone try to rebuke them. Instead, they do one of the many more natural things to do such as pitying themselves over their hurt, calling other people and informing them about the offender and their bad mannerisms, and getting furious and worked up enough that even if they were to go to the offender, the motive would not be to rebuke them but to "talk some" sense into them." A typical response by brothers and sisters to offenses committed against them—especially by fellow brethren—is usually less confrontational but still not what Jesus commanded. These brethren may go about warning other brethren to be wary of the behavior of the offending brother lest they come to the same or similar hurt. Many times, this is carefully concealed to look like a form of testimony to other brethren or a concern that the brother or sister shares with others to help them keep out of harm's way.

The reality is that this is not what Jesus commanded. Even though the approach may seem outwardly right—and also to the other brethren who may respond by keeping off the errant brother and saving themselves from similar or more severe harm—doing this would not help the situation. Instead, it would compound it and make the offending person more likely to be subjected to scorn and injury. That is why Jesus demands explicitly that the offended person finds the offender and, having seen him, rebukes him. Therefore, the first step of this three-step process toward forgiveness would be for the offended person to take the right action, namely going to find the offender. He meant that once the offender was found, the offended person would gently tell the person about the offense without using any harsh language or a confrontational style.

Being gentle is the key here. Jesus did not ask the offender to go telling other people about the offense in the name of what Christians would make out to appear like a testimony. He did not require that the offended person sit somewhere and feel sorry for themselves for the offense or to take the whole matter to the other person and turn the anger outwardly toward other innocent people or pets. Instead, the command is for the offended person to go to the offended. This is why it has been argued that it is the obligation of the offended person—not that of the offender—to go to the offender. It is true that in a different passage of scripture, Jesus demanded that the offender go and be reconciled with their brother whom they have wronged before they can give their offering to God. Otherwise, the offering would not be accepted:

> Therefore, if you are offering your gift at the altar and there remember that your brother or sister has something against you, leave your gift there in front of the altar. First, go and be reconciled to them; then come and offer your gift.[134]

Therefore, there are commands for the offender and the offended person to go meet up with each other and seek to be reconciled. The critical issue in this regard, then, seems to be the need for reconciliation or forgiveness and regardless of who takes the initiative first. Still, the command in Luke is very specific that the offended person should find the offender and not necessarily be reconciled with him but rebuke him. In going, the offended person does not look for reconciliation but is instead looking to give a rebuke to the offender. The two passages of scripture diverge in these two regards.

## The Hurt, Hate, Hook, and Heal Process of Forgiving

Forgiveness could also take place through a slightly different process but with virtually the same fundamental processes and outcomes. This process starts with the hurt and then proceeds to the hate and hook before moving on to the healing methods. Even before examining each of these individual phases or operations, it can be noted at this point that of the three, the one that is without a doubt most important is the processes of healing.

---

[134] Matthew 5:23–24 NIV.

It will be a waste of time and emotional investments into the forgiveness processes if the forgiving person does not heal from the processes. Actually, the ultimate goal of forgiveness should be the total healing of the offended person as well as the deliverance from the negative feelings of resentment and bitterness. Those feelings waste away the bones and crush the spirit, resulting in a physically, emotionally, and even mentally ill person. This is why healing has to be given priority, and by extension, this is why the process of forgiveness needs to be completed (as explained in chapter 6).

## 1. The Hurt Phase: The Need to Identify, Experience, and Express the Hurt

Any process of forgiveness has to be commensurate with the identification of the hurt. Without first identifying the hurt, forgiveness may not become complete. It is arguable whether forgiveness would be needed in the first place if the offended person cannot identify the hurt or if there is no hurt. A major problem or challenge in this regard is that many people pretend they have not been hurt or that even though they were initially hurt, the hurt is no longer present. People may overcome the pain over time, depending on the magnitude of the offense. Truth be told, all offenses hurt, but they do not hurt equally or in the same way. Some offenses hurt more than others, depending on, among other factors, the attitude of the person who committed the offense, the perceived gravity or severity of the offense based on societal norms and customs, the perceived justification for the offense, and the response of the offender to the offense.

Even if an offense is mostly regarded as minor in society, the hurt it causes to the offended person could be magnified if the offender is indifferent to the offense or if the offender is not willing to apologize. On the other hand, the hurt caused by an offense perceived by society to be grave could significantly diminish the resultant harm if the offended person feels that he or she did something that caused the offense or played a key role in the response. Notwithstanding these factors, the fact of the matter is that every offense is associated with a specific hurt. Therefore, it really ought not to matter the magnitude or severity of the harm because any form of pain is enough to require healing. Thus, one of the most critical approaches to the process of forgiveness is to identify the hurt.

Another critical aspect pertaining to the hurt phase of forgiveness is the experience. In this regard, the offended person needs to allow themselves to relive and reexperience the hurt as was felt. This may seem farfetched or even counterproductive, but it is an important aspect, especially if healing from the offense is to be realized (and true forgiveness achieved). The hurt has to be the expression of the deep feelings linked to the pain. The offended person's experiences and feelings are just as meaningful as being able to identify the hurt. In fact, identification of the damage almost always leads to experiencing and expressing emotions. However, this may not happen in cases where the person deliberately covers up feelings for reasons such as fear of being accused of not forgiving or feigning forgiveness.

More often than not, offended people do not want to be seen as holding on to the hurt of negative feelings of resentment, anger, and bitterness. For them, being seen as holding on to these feelings and emotions is an indication that the offense still hurts them. Since many people do not want to be regarded as being negatively affected by a given offense, they simulate attitudes and feelings of happiness and calmness. Granted an opportunity, they may even deny having been hurt in any way. Unfortunately, such attempts to cover up offenses and their resultant hurts are more common among born-again Christians than nonbelievers. This is because Christians, by the nature of their calling and faith, tend to be quite sensitive to how they treat other people and how they look (or appear) to fellow brethren.

The admission that a given past offense hurts is often interpreted as a sign of weakness or even failure. As a result, offended people will try to cover up the true extent of their hurt without realizing that doing this only stands in the way of forgiveness and healing. It is akin to a patient who goes to the doctor and gives misleading symptoms instead of openly answering the physician's questions and revealing their true feelings. The result is usually a misdiagnosis and the negative consequences associated with it. Otherwise, the patient will not be able to heal as fast as if they had given the correct symptoms of the condition being experienced.

Christians, in particular, tend to be extremely hesitant to reveal the true extent of their hurt, especially if they have been hurt by someone close to them, someone they consider to be superior to them, or someone with spiritual authority over them. For instance, a sister who has been offended by a male church leader or even the pastor may be extremely secretive about the whole issue. This is part of the natural tendency to want to protect the image of the church and its leadership. Normally, exposing such an offense—and the associated hurt—risks breaking up the entire church and scattering the flock. The offended person is concerned that revealing how much she was hurt could, in the end, result in the speculation of the magnitude of the offense even if the actual attack is not disclosed. Therefore, the person may decide to act as though nothing severe happened or that something offensive happened but that she has since gotten past it.

While it is sometimes essential for the reputation of the church to be protected, this ought not to be done at the expense of believers' pain and emotional hurt. Instead, the offended person needs to be courageous enough to reveal the extent of the harm, even if she fails to explain the offender or the nature of the offense. The person needs to identify, experience clearly, and express her feelings about the offense. If she thinks the church leaders are hypocrites because one of them gossiped about her, then she is justified to do that for the sake of the process of forgiveness. The hurt phase of the process of forgiving is designed to help the offended person ventilate and realize (and appreciate) that there is bottled-up anger inside of them. Letting out this anger and replacing it with a patient and calm spirit, which results from forgiving, is the ultimate goal of this process.

The offended person is required not just to be able to clearly and accurately identify their feelings but also to experience and express those feelings. Labeling these feelings in the most specific detail possible is critical because it helps ensure that every emotion is identified, accounted for, experienced, and expressed. This, in turn, entails deliberately thinking back to the offense as a whole and also the events leading to or possibly triggering the offense hurt and the associated feelings of bitterness, engager, perhaps even revenge. Thinking back to what caused the feelings is no less important than identifying the emotions and experiencing and expressing them. Among other issues, the offender may need to identify the person who offended them, when the offense occurred, and the place or setting where it all happened. The ability to do this will significantly enhance the chances of the offended person forgiving the person. On the contrary, missing one or more of these issues and events that led to the hurt may stand in the way of genuine forgiveness.

For instance, unless the offended person can identify the person or people who offended them, it would be hard to forgive. Forgiveness can be directed at unknown people as happens when someone hurts another anonymously. While driving on a busy expressway, for instance, it is not unusual for one to be cut off by unknown or unidentifiable drivers. However, the person still gets offended or hurt as a result of the incident. In such instances, forgiving has to be done without the knowledge of who did it. Even then, there is still a need for as much information about the incident as possible to be remembered in order to facilitate the identification, experience, and expression of feelings.

## 2. The Hate Phase: Confessing the Hate

The second phase in this process is the one dealing with the hate of the offense. The hurt is vital in the process of forgiving; hate is also essential. If the pain of the process is hard for many people to acknowledge or admit, then the hatred is even harder. People usually do not want to be associated with negative emotions or feelings, primarily if these feelings are directed at a person who is close to them or a fellow Christian. It is not unusual for everyone in the church to want to look as perfect and as close to God as they can be. On Sundays in particular, everyone puts on an air of holiness that makes them look as though they have had nothing to do with sin all week long or even all their lives. It is a portrayal of human beings' desire to be perfect and acceptable before God, something that can only be achieved when they resist the devil and do not sin.

However, there is a difference between resisting the evil one and not sinning. Just because Satan is resisted, it does not mean that one is free from sin. It is written that believers ought to resist the devil: "Submit yourselves, then, to God. Resist the devil, and he will flee from you."[135] However, there are times when believers are overcome with temptation, which ultimately leads to sin:

---

[135] James 4:7 NIV.

Let no man say when he is tempted, I am tempted of God: for God cannot be tempted with evil, neither tempteth he any man: But every man is tempted, when he is drawn away of his own lust, and enticed. Then when lust hath conceived, it bringeth forth sin: and sin, when it is finished, bringeth forth death.[136]

Everyone has some not-so-godly desires from time to time, and this means that no one is immune to sin:

For all have sinned, and come short of the glory of God; Being justified freely by his grace through the redemption that is in Christ Jesus.[137]

God commendeth his love toward us, in that, while we were yet sinners, Christ died for us.[138]

Therefore, every person is prone to sinning, and if there is any trace of perfection in believers, it is because Christ has atoned for those sins.

Therefore, it is a reality that no person is without sin. This is, in turn, the basis for contending that there is nothing wrong with an offended person admitting to having harbored—or still harboring—hate toward the offender. After all, this is how it is supposed to happen: hate naturally follows hurt. While some people do hate others without necessarily being hurt, hardly ever, if at all, will anyone hate another without being damaged. It all comes down to how the two people involved in the offense think of and perceive the incident. Some, especially the offenders, may think it was not worth the resultant hate, and others, especially the offended people, almost always feel the hurt was far deeper compared to the hatred being manifested as a result.

Therefore, in the second phase, the offended person is required to exhibit hate. However, this does not mean that the offender is to be hated, which is the desire of many angry people. The reality is that it is far easier

---

[136] James 1:13–15 KJV.
[137] Romans 3:23–24 KJV.
[138] Romans 5:8 KJV.

to hate the person who has made another person hurt deeply. That is how human beings have been wired to respond. In fact, hating the person seems to be the lesser evil in this regard because there are usually greater evils that can follow, such as paying back the person by doing precisely the same thing to them or even physically attacking the person. Hate is mostly regarded as a safer way of dealing with the offense. This ought not to mean that hate is a positive emotion or feeling that should be encouraged except in a few limited circumstances, and hate tends to be even more lethal than physical confrontations, primarily when it is directed at the offending person as opposed to the offense or the wrong thing done.

In this regard, hate is not wrong, and God himself requires believers to hate whatever he hates. For instance, God expects his people to hate sin and all the appearance of evil:

> Prove all things; hold fast that which is good. Abstain from all appearance of evil.[139]

However, he does not ask his people to hate those who sin against them or who do wrong to them. The hate has to be directed at the wrongdoing and not the doer of the wrong. The sinner is to be loved in spite of the sin, which is the one to be hated. This distinction is essential. Most of the time, offended people hate their offenders, and this often stands in the way of forgiveness. This happens when the hate prevents the offended person from releasing the offender from the expectation that the offender will ever repay the offended person for the hurt caused. The offended person may need to be assisted in making this critical distinction, especially given the tendency by offended people not to calm down enough to be able to think objectively.

Even when the offended person is the one who is usually knowledgeable about God's expectations about hating, not the sinner but the sin, the anger, and the hate of the moment could cloud this rational thinking and cause them to hate the sinner instead. If hatred is directed at the sinner rather than the sin, it is unlikely that forgiveness would result because it would then mean that the offended person may not be willing and ready

---

[139] 1 Thessalonians 5:21–22 KJV.

to release the person. The goal in this phase of the forgiveness process ought to be ensuring that the offended person has the right sense of mind to understand that even though hating is necessary—even important—it has to be directed at the offense. This way, the offended person may later be more inclined to release the offender even if he or she does not let go of the offense.

This is why it is not always a good thing to require offended people to forget as part of the forgiving process. Many are the times when forgiving is followed by forgetting. However, forgetting ought to never be a requirement for forgiving. Subsequently, offenders need not be made to forget the offense as an indication of having forgiven. Instead, they are at liberty to remember the offense for as long as they want. All they should not do is direct their hate and anger at the offender once forgiveness has taken place.

The offended person will also need to confess to their hatred as part of the process of forgiving—and not as a way of judging them. When people refuse to confess their deep-seated anger or gloss over it and act as though it means nothing, there is a great danger that the person may not forgive. True forgiveness requires openness, sincerity, and a willingness to admit that hate is there. After all, forgiving is partly letting go of the hate. Therefore, denial of the existence of any hate—or minimizing the effect of the hate—may be counterproductive. Actually, it is a reality that when persistent hatred is bottled up and not confessed, it can lead to more serious emotional and even mental problems, such as depression. It is usually not worth getting depressed as a result of someone's offense. This is why it is highly recommended that offended people resist holding onto the hate and resentment, especially for an extended period of time. The more they hold onto hate, the more harm they cause themselves—and not the offender.

If anything, the offender usually has no knowledge that he or she offended someone; if there is such knowledge, the offender has little or no care about it. This is why confession of the hate is essential.

James asked believers to confess their sins to one another:

> Confess your faults one to another, and pray one for another, that ye may be healed [because] the effectual fervent prayer of a righteous man availeth much.[140]

This further underscores the importance of confessing one's hatred for the offender and, in doing so, getting the opportunity to redirect the hostility to the right target: the offense. James must have had the foreknowledge that when sins are not confessed, they cause health problems (or they are the problems themselves). That is why he directly linked the confession of sins to healing.

As has been noted, depression is an extreme condition that can result from prolonged and persistent hatred that is not being confessed. Evidently, it is much better to acknowledge than to be afflicted with all kinds of emotional and psychological disorders occasioned by bottled-up negative emotions such as anger, hatred, and resentment. Forgiveness helps the offended person and not the offender because forgiveness takes place within the heart and mind of the offended person. Even if the offender is present, he or she may not benefit from the emotional release and healing since he or she is not the one who had these bottled-up negative emotions in the first place. If there are any benefits to the offender, they are usually shared between the offender and the offended person and not only for the offender.

This is one more reason why offended people need to be at the forefront in forgiving their offenders. The offended people get healing as a result of the confession of their sins. The offender may confess one's sins to God—or even to the offended person—and receive the same kind of healing that James talked about in scripture. However, the offender is usually not in need of doing the type of confession discussed in this specific context because the offender hardly ever, if at all, holds onto hatred for the offended person. Instead, he or she tends to move on once the offense has been committed. The kind of confession discussed in this context is that whereby the offended person admits to having harbored negative emotions—including hatred—a result of the offense. In this regard, this is the kind of confession that results in healing.

---

[140] James 5:16 KJV.

## 3. The Hook Phase: Acknowledgement of the Deceptive Feeling of Control

Refusing to forgive provides a feeling of power, but this feeling is usually deceptive and not true or accurate. In fact, there is typically no way the offended person has control over the offender. It is just a false sense of control. Therefore, the third phase in this particular process of forgiveness is the need to acknowledge and deal with this deceptive feeling of power to which one can be firmly hooked. In this case, the hook refers to the false impression of control onto which the offended person tends to hold for as long as possible.

As was noted before in this book, the offended person seems to have some kind of authority or control over the offender. This control or sense of power has stood in the way of forgiveness for so many people over so many years because few people seem ready, willing, and able to let go of that feeling. This is mostly because they think that for as long as they have this feeling, they genuinely have control and authority over the offender. Deep inside, they want and crave this control as a way of making sure the offender remains captive to them.

Everyone who has ever been offended—and it is practically everyone who has ever lived in this world for at least several years—knows that forgiving becomes hard because of the fear and insecurity associated with the unknown. One seems not sure what will happen next when one lets go of this feeling of power. In the field of political science, a shared philosophy is that absolute power corrupts absolutely. This phrase is relevant in this regard because this feeling of control is false and not real, and it has the same effect of damaging the offended person. Even if the corruption is not absolute, it is significant enough to make the person act in antisocial ways and deviate from what is usually expected of them. This happens because the offender is trying to exhibit actually nonexistent power. In reality, the offender is attempting to conceal their own sense of hurt and the associated vulnerability.

Offended people are usually in the habit of thinking that the offender is likely to hurt them again. The deeper the hurt they experienced as a result of the offense, the more likely they are to think the offender is up to no good and may hurt them again. This explains the false power play that is a strategy or way of preventing the hurt from occurring and manifesting.

Being offended is profoundly hurting, yet few people want to have their hurting experiences be known by everyone. Therefore, they do all that is practically possible within their limited abilities to deflect the situation away from themselves and onto the offender. If listened to carefully, such people may use statements such as "How could they do something like that to me?" "I think my being good and kind is being taken advantage of by people and mistaken for weakness," "He will go nowhere until he comes to me and begs for mercy," or "What were they even thinking when they crossed my path? They will know who I am."

The same people, when asked if they have forgiven their offenders, will most likely be quick to claim they did so a long time ago. A few may admit to not being ready to forgive, but even such ones may claim that they have nothing against the person and therefore see no need to forgive. These are usually the signs that the people concerned are still far from forgiving because they are still hooked to their false sense of power. When people make such statements or use such words, it is usually indicative of the fact that they have been deeply hurt but are doing everything in their power to cover up their own sense of hurt and vulnerability. It shows that they feel exposed and vulnerable to their offenders, and letting go of these feelings of power would take away whatever limited defense mechanisms they may have against the offender.

The other way to describe the false sense of power is that they are actually victims of the offense and are therefore in need of being helped. It is hard enough to be offended and hurt by someone, but it becomes even harder when one becomes a victim of either the offender or the offense. Being a victim of the offense means that one holds onto the offense and does not readily let go. They approach and regard the offense from the perspective of being in control or having power over it when, in reality, the offense and the offender have power over them.

Therefore, one of the essential steps that offended people can take if they are to forgive from their hearts is to reject the tremendous and overwhelming desire to become victims. Whenever they feel that they have control of or power over the situation or the other people, they have to resist this feeling because it is usually false. An excellent way to do this is to admit any feelings of vulnerability and deep hurt instead of attempting to cover them up. Covering up vulnerabilities and the damages results false feelings of power and control over the offender.

Having refused to be victims, offended people may need to make the conscious choice to cancel the debt.[141] As was noted earlier in this book, forgiveness means cancellation of a unique kind of debt, which involves releasing the offender from the expectation that he or she will be able to pay for the hurt or harm caused to the offended person. The offended people have to know that there is indeed a debt that is, humanly speaking, due to them. This is the debt owed as a result of the hurt caused by the offender. Having known so, they ought to move forward and understand that even though they are owed by their offenders, they need to let go of the debt because God desires that no person is indebted to any other:

> Render therefore to all their dues: a tribute to whom tribute is due; custom to whom custom; fear to whom fear; honor to whom honor. Owe no man anything, but to love one another: for he that loveth another hath fulfilled the law.[142]

The only debt that is permissible before God is the continuing and, therefore, the endless debt of love. God expects people to owe others love just as other people also owe them love. As a result, people have to extend love to each other if not for anything else than for the sake of God. After all, it is only when one loves one's brother that a person can truly claim to love God. This issue of loving fellow people as a sign of loving God is the central message in John's first epistle:

> We love him, because he first loved us. If a man says, I love God, and hateth his brother, he is a liar: for he that loveth not his brother whom he hath seen, how can he love God whom he hath not seen? And this commandment have

---

[141] June Hunt, *Biblical Counseling Keys on Forgiveness: The Freedom to Let Go* (Dallas, TX: Hope for The Heart, 2008), 23.

[142] Romans 13:7–8 KJV.

we from him, That he who loveth God love his brother also.[143]

It is upon this love for their fellow brothers, including their offenders, that offended people need to base their forgiveness. Without love, there can be no forgiveness of sins because love leads to giving—and giving leads to forgiving:

> God demonstrates his own love for us in this: While we were still sinners, Christ died for us.[144]

> God so loved the world that he gave his one and only Son, that whoever believes in him shall not perish but have eternal life. For God did not send his Son into the world to condemn the world but to save the world through him.[145]

> In fact, the law requires that nearly everything is cleansed with blood, and without the shedding of blood there is no forgiveness [of sin].[146]

It is only when offenders realize and appreciate that it is a sin against God to not love other people that they may be inclined to love those who have offended them. As a result of this love, they may be more willing to cancel and let go of any owed debts, including the emotional debts owed as a result of the hurt caused by their offenders. Therefore, canceling the debt is vital if forgiveness is to take place.

However, forgiveness does not end with canceling the debt. Instead, there is a lot more that needs to be done to make the process complete. As is emphasized in the next chapter, completing the process of forgiveness is just as important as starting it because unless the process is completed, forgiveness may not really result in the desired outcomes for the offender. Therefore, cancellation of the debt is to be followed by the deliberate

---

[143] 1 John 4:19–21 KJV.
[144] Romans 5:8 NIV.
[145] John 3:16–17 NIV.
[146] Hebrews 9:22 NIV.

decision to move on with one's life. This is an important issue because people who have been offended and have refused to cancel their offenders' debts seem not to live their lives at all. Instead, their lives seem to be dependent on and dictated by the offense and resultant hurt. Therefore, they may go on talking about the offense and the pain and virtually everything about what happened to them. While such talk may be necessary for the early phase of the process of forgiveness, a time comes when the person has to cease talking about the past and the offenses and make the deliberate decision to move on with life.

This is where a determination can be made regarding the person who has genuinely canceled the debts owed to them by offenders and those people who are only pretending to have canceled the debts when they have not. People who have canceled debts owed to them are more likely to move on much faster than their counterparts who still hold on the debts and want the debts to be repaid. As expected, both categories of people will readily admit to having canceled the debts owed to them, which is part of the cover up mentioned earlier. This, in turn, shows just how much of a struggle it can be to decide not to hold the offender accountable for the offense and the hurt caused. It is akin to forgiving a substantial monetary or financial debt owed by a person or an institution.

For example, consider how hard it usually is to cancel a debt that a person owes a bank. The larger the debt, the harder it often is to for anyone to cancel the debt. It becomes even harder for the debt to be canceled when the debtor is arrogant and is merely refusing to pay even though they can repay it. Surely, all financial institutions have the capacity to pay the debts they owe to individual investors or creditors. However, for such ones, failure to pay is usually a deliberate act and not one caused by a lack of funds. The same applies to forgiveness, where offenders typically can facilitate the process of forgiveness. Many are simply not willing or are unavailable since they are not hurt by the continuation of the debt, but those they owe are. Still, cancellation of debt has to be followed by the decision to move on with life instead of being stuck in the past. Moving on in this regard means that their past offenses no longer define the lives of the offended people. Instead, the offense is now in the past and, where possible, forgotten.

The relationship with the offenders may also be reestablished if this is possible, but this is not mandatory because it depends on the offended people and their offenders. If the rebuilding of past relationships was a priority for both parties, it has to take place at this stage where the relationship goes back to what it used to be or even becomes better. Also, if there is no reestablishment of the past relationship, the offended people must still be able to focus on living their lives irrespective of their present and previous contact with the offender.

As part of the process of moving on with life, offended people may need to let God be the one to bring justice in their situations:

> Good and upright is the Lord: therefore, will he teach sinners in the way. The meek will he guide in judgment: and the meek will he teach his way.[147]

> It is mine to avenge; I will repay. In due time their foot will slip; their day of disaster is near, and their doom rushes upon them.[148]

This does not necessarily mean that the offended people have to ask God to repay their offenders as their offenses deserve. God does not act like that or even answer prayers of that nature. Instead, God is pleased with people who pray for their enemies and do good to those who offend them:

> Ye have heard that it hath been said, Thou shalt love thy neighbor, and hate thine enemy. But I say unto you, Love your enemies, bless them that curse you, do good to them that hate you, and pray for them which despitefully use you, and persecute you; That ye may be the children of your Father which is in heaven: for he maketh his sun to rise on the evil and on the good, and sendeth rain on the just and on the unjust.[149]

Therefore, even in letting God take over the situation, offended people

---

[147] Psalm 25:8–9 KJV.
[148] Deuteronomy 32:35 NIV.
[149] Matthew 5:43–45 KJV.

ought to guard against the tendency to wish that harm came the way of their offenders. It is only human to feel that way, and denying this feeling is sometimes an indication of a person who is not ready to move on with life after forgiving or after releasing an offender from the expectation that the offender will ever be able to repay them for the offense committed and hurt caused. Allowing God into the situation instead means that the offended people trust God to make right everything that is not right about the situation. It is about letting God's will take precedence over personal will in the matter.

In this regard, forgiving could be said to be letting go of and letting God. While vengeance seems like the right and only reasonable thing to do when one has been deeply hurt, it also hardly ever works. In essence, revenge hardly ever helps offended people achieve their goals. Instead, it only leads to more destruction because it encourages engagement in self-destructive behavior. Specifically, revenge seeks to pay back the offender using the same type or form of hurt caused. For instance, revenge will tell a person whose spouse engaged in an extramarital affair to also engage in an extramarital relationship. Giving the offender "a dose of their own medicine" seems like the right and plausible thing to do. In this case, however, the offender will never be able to experience as much hurt, pain, and suffering from the affair as if the spouse had an affair as the pain, hurt, and suffering experienced by the offended person.

In fact, the offender may experience no pain at all because it is unlikely that they have found out about the affair. Even if they found out about the affair of their spouse, there are chances that they were expecting it all along anyway and would therefore neither be surprised nor hurt by it. The end result would be a situation where one spouse was deeply troubled by the infidelity of the other and also decides to engage in a similar affair to get revenge. However, the first spouse finds this revenge usual or even amusing and continues with the affair. The hurting spouse only gets hurt even more. Besides, the offended spouse now has just made an otherwise complex difficult situation more complicated and complex by engaging in an affair against their will. Ultimately, the pain supposedly given out to the offending spouse hardly ever matches the pain received—let alone cancels out the pain received.

Every action or inaction has consequences for those concerned. It is possible for offended people to feel relieved when they pay back the offender for the offense committed and the pain suffered or being experienced. This makes them quite satisfied or even happy.[150] However, such satisfaction and happiness, if it ever comes, is usually short-lived and hardly ever is about the ultimate desired outcome of getting even. Truth be told, there is practically no way that human beings can get even with each other because they are, by nature, limited in their abilities and what they can do.

Only God can even up matters for everyone and make any situation good for everyone concerned. Many times, in the Bible, it is written, with a lot of emphasis, that nothing is impossible with God. Therefore, it is best if offended people choose to follow the seemingly difficult way of allowing God to take over the situation instead of choosing the seemingly easier way out by taking revenge. In the end, it is the former way that always works. This is why it is highly advisable for offended people to let go of their resentment and pain and let God take care of the situation as only he can. After all, God is omnipotent, omniscient, and omnipresent, and he understands everything.[151]

God sees things differently from the way human beings see things:

> But the Lord said to Samuel, "Do not consider his appearance or his height, for I have rejected him. The Lord does not look at the things people look at. People look at the outward appearance, but the Lord looks at the heart.[152]

While God looks at people's hearts and weighs their motivations, human beings look at things from the outside. In matters of forgiveness, it is better to examine hearts than to go by outward feelings and emotions, which can be quite deceptive. Outwardly, the pain caused by the hurt seems impossible and only worth sharing with the offender through revenge. Inwardly, however, God most likely sees an offended person

[150] Larry D. Ellis, *Forgiveness: Unleashing a Transformational Process* (Denver, CO: Adoration Publishing Company, 2010), 39.
[151] Psalm 139:1–24 NIV.
[152] 1 Samuel 16:7 NIV.

who is deeply hurt and who needs to release the offender from the debt of having to pay for the offense or the hurt caused.

Luckily for everyone in such a situation, God is ready and willing to help them:

> Come unto me, all ye that labor and are heavy laden, and
> I will give you rest.[153]

Going to God instead of to the offender or other people is the surest way to overcome the pain, forget the past, let go of the debt, and move on with life.

## 4. The Heal Phase: Going Through the Process of Healing

The fourth and final phase of the process of forgiveness is healing. This is arguably one of the essential phases in the process of forgiveness because unless offended, total healing from the hurts and pain caused by the offense's forgiveness may never take place. If forgiveness did take place, it was incomplete. Forgiving is worth its name if it is complete—and all the necessary processes and steps are completed satisfactorily.

It is worth adding that forgiving could be regarded as an event or a process depending on the aspects that one seeks to emphasize. Therefore, it is best to consider forgiveness as both a process and an event. Forgiveness is merely an event to the offender because they are only receiving the forgiveness from the offended person. Everyone who has ever had to accept anything knows that it needs not take more than a moment. It is merely an exchange that takes seconds or a minutes. Ceremonies held or words exchanged may be said as part of the dialogue, but in the end, the actual exchange only takes a few seconds or minutes. The same happens when the offended person grants forgiveness to the offender. However, forgiveness becomes a process when—or at the point which—the offended person has to find relief from the pain suffered. Clearly, it is much easier to forgive than it is to heal from the hurt caused by the offense. It is therefore not surprising that granting forgiveness to the offender is short-lived, is

---

[153] Matthew 11:28 KJV.

comfortable, and is an event while getting relief from the pain suffered takes time, is difficult, and is a process.

Because healing is a process and takes time, there should be a deliberate choice on the part of offended people to ensure that they have adequate time to heal from their hurts.[154] This is another extremely difficult phase of the process of forgiving because of the tendency of offended people to minimize or underrate its importance. Partly because of the need to be seen by other people to have forgiven the offender and moved on with life and partly because of not understanding the value of true healing, many offended people are in a rush to complete this stage—and hardly ever go through it. If they do go through it, many want to make it an event as opposed to the process it is meant to be. Therefore, it is not totally unusual for offended people being taken through the process of forgiveness to approach their pastor and ask to be prayed for in order to "heal" from the hurt. Honestly, many pastors have gone ahead and prayed for the people just as they have asked. They may say, "Loving father, heal your son/daughter from their past hurts." Afterward, these people might go away and "feel" healed.

This is not supposed to be an indictment of pastors who are most committed to their work and do everything in their capacity to help people heal from their past hurts, which are a result from being offended. Instead, it is supposed to highlight an mostly overlooked yet important issue in the process of healing: time. Without adequate time to heal, the most potent and faithful prayers made by the most powerful "man or woman of God" may never bring about healing. James gave specific instructions for how sick people ought to approach their sickness in order to be healed:

> Is any sick among you? Let him call for the elders of the church; and let them pray over him, anointing him with oil in the name of the Lord: And the prayer of faith shall

---

[154] Robert Jeffress, *When Forgiveness Doesn't Make Sense* (Colorado Springs, CO: WaterBrook, 2000), 47.

save the sick, and the Lord shall raise him up; and if he has committed sins, they shall be forgiven him.[155]

Subsequently, it seems a reasonable and usual thing to do for people with different kinds of sickness to approach church elders to be prayed for. However, the kind of healing involved in forgiveness is not the same as the healing that James was talking about. While the apostle was talking about healing from physical ailments or sicknesses, the kind of healing required in the process of forgiveness is mostly emotional and psychological. While everything is possible before God—and every illness can without question be healed by God—it is the same God who provided human beings with the knowledge of time. Therefore, God must have understood the value of time in the total healing of specific ailments.

Moreover, God has different ways of healing people and does not always use the method of prayer. Jesus would pray for some and ask others to take some action. For instance, God (via the prophet Elisha) required Naaman to dip himself in the Jordan River seven times to be healed:

> Elisha sent a messenger to say to [Naaman], "Go, wash yourself seven times in the Jordan, and your flesh will be restored and you will be cleansed." So he went down and dipped himself in the Jordan seven times, as the man of God had told him, and his flesh was restored and became clean like that of a young boy.[156]

Clearly, Naaman did not expect that in order to be healed, he needed to go dip himself in the dirty and raging waters of the River Jordan. Instead, like many other people of his time, he must have expected that the prophet would simply lay his hands on him—and then he would be well. However, that is not how God works. God is always concerned with

---

[155] James 5:14–15. KJV. "Prophet Uebert Angel Biography: Best of Christianity." Accessed December 14, 2019. https://bestofchristianity.com/prophet-uebert-angel-biography-wife-children-books-age-ministry-net-worth-children-house-cars-private-jets-and-contact-details/.

[156] "2 Kings 5:10: Elisha Sent a Messenger to Say to Him, 'Go, Was...'" Bible Study Tools. Accessed November 11, 2019. https://www.biblestudytools.com/2-kings/5-10.html.

the attitude of the person seeking to be healed. He is mainly interested in the faith of the person. Once God establishes that a person has faith, the method used to bring about healing seems to be of little significance to him. Jesus healed some people by covering their eyes with mud, and he healed others by merely ordering them to get up, take their mats, and go. Still, other people were healed by simply being spoken to by Jesus's commands: "Arise, go, your faith has made you whole."[157] Still, he healed others by laying hands on them. The bottom line is that God is unlimited in terms of the methods he used to bring about healing.

Therefore, offended people ought not to always expect that they can only receive healing by being prayed for in a certain way. When it comes to healing from emotional wounds, it really matters which method is adopted, but it has to take time and be a process as opposed to an event. It is okay if offended people choose to seek prayers from church elders or even their pastors. However, this is unlikely to help them as much as allowing themselves time to heal slowly and naturally. Time is the ultimate healer of the deepest wounds.

---

[157] Luke 19:9 NIV.

# CHAPTER 6

# THE BENEFITS OF COMPLETING THE PROCESS OF FORGIVING

One of the reasons why forgiveness is difficult is because it takes time and goes through a long, often drawn-out, process[158] as was illustrated in the preceding chapter. Yet, it is paramount that the offended person, in particular, goes through the entire process if any benefits are to be realized. Leaving the process midway may leave the offended person with some baggage that may still negatively affect their life. When all the stages are completed—in a satisfactory manner—the offended people are able to wake up someday and discover that they have totally changed how they think about the people who hurt them. Often, it will be a change from having bitter thoughts to feelings virtually healthy, calm, and even happy when thinking about the offender, the offense, and the hurt caused by the offense.[159] It is a sort of radical transformation that everyone needs to undergo, given the fact that all people offend and have been offended. Therefore, the process of forgiveness needs to be undertaken and completed.

The other benefit associated with completing the process of forgiveness is that even if the offended people end up disliking or distrusting their

---

[158] Larry D. Ellis, *Forgiveness: Unleashing a Transformational Process* (Denver, CO: Adoration Publishing Company, 2010), 11.

[159] Robert Jeffress, *When Forgiveness Doesn't Make Sense* (Colorado Springs, CO: WaterBrook, 2000), 49.

offenders, the intensity of their hurt will definitely diminish significantly when the process has been completed. They may find themselves more at ease when the people are mentioned in conversations or when they meet. This chapter discusses the benefits associated with completing the process of forgiveness. In this regard, this is one of the most critical sections in the book because failure to complete the process of forgiveness is, in many ways, tantamount to not forgiving at all. Yet when the process is followed to completion, many benefits are realizable.

## Praying for the Offender

Sometimes the offended people may find themselves actually praying—deliberately or subconsciously—for the people who offended them. Among other things, being able to actually pray for one's offender is a sign that the offended person has successfully completed the process of forgiveness.

If forgiving is hard, it is partly because it requires offended people to pray for their offenders instead of cursing them:

> I say unto you, "Love your enemies, bless them that curse you, do good to them that hate you, and pray for them which despitefully use you, and persecute you."[160]

When offended people get to the point where they find themselves not struggling to pray for their offenders, they have really managed to complete the process of forgiveness. Praying for the offender, as used in the Bible, does not necessarily mean making long and extended prayers as would happen in church. Instead, it simply means being able to commit the person before God in prayer and ask God to bless them and do well for them.

Forgiving is usually difficult because offended people think they have been commanded—and are therefore under obligation—to pray for their offenders. This command may seem easy from the face of it, especially for those who do not take prayer seriously or do not really understand the true meaning of praying for someone. The place of prayer is a sacred place, and it is where a person meets their God. During prayer, men and women pour

---

[160] Matthew 5:44 KJV.

their souls out to God and hold nothing back. They make every aspect of their lives known to God and petition God to have his way in their lives.

Simply put, there is no pretense or hypocrisy in the place of prayer. Instead, people are serious and committed and truly surrender their wills to the will of the only God who is able to do immeasurably more than what we can ask.[161]

So important is prayer in the sight of God that Jesus took time to teach his disciples how to pray:

> And he said unto them, When ye pray, say, Our Father which art in heaven, Hallowed be thy name. Thy kingdom come. Thy will be done, as in heaven, so in earth. Give us day by day our daily bread. And forgive us our sins; for we also forgive every one that is indebted to us. And lead us not into temptation; but deliver us from evil.[162]

James also wrote about the importance of confession and prayer:

> Confess *your* faults one to another, and pray one for another, that ye may be healed. The effectual fervent prayer of a righteous man availeth much.[163]

Since prayer makes much available or avails much, it is essential when an offended person is able to pay for the offender since this shows that true forgiveness has taken place. Only a person who has genuinely forgiven an offender can sincerely want the offender to receive God's blessings. Since prayer makes God open the floodgates of heaven and release his blessings, those who pray for their offenders are, in effect, keen to see God's blessings in their offenders' lives. This shows genuine forgiveness. Usually, offended people will ask for the exact opposite—curses—to be channeled to their offenders. After all, it only feels right to do that in light of the fact that offenders cause so much hurt and harm to their victims.

---

[161] Ephesians 3:20 NIV.

[162] Luke 11:2–4 KJV.

[163] James 5:16 KJV.

Therefore, the process of forgiveness can only be said to be complete if the offended person no longer seeks "an eye for an eye" or "a tooth for a tooth" and instead repays good for evil. Everyone knows how hard it is to return good for evil. It is just not human nature to do that.[164] Forgiving is difficult because it requires doing something good in exchange for the wrong things done to a person.

The most critical issue is that prayer is not easy—even when it is done for oneself. If Jesus's disciples could not know how to pray, one can only expect that ordinary people, especially if they are not believers, will find prayer extremely difficult. People may want to pray to God for something, but they are forced not to do so because they have no idea how to pray. If people cannot pray for themselves—for things that are of importance and benefit to themselves—then they cannot be expected to pray for those who offend them or their debtors. It is a command and not a choice for all those who have been hurt to pray for their offenders and do good to them. This is not something that anyone can claim to enjoy or look forward to since it is extremely difficult.

It is usually much easier for people to say that they will pray for their enemies, but in reality, many hardly ever do it. As a result, the phrases "I will pray for you" or "I am praying for you" have become cliché, even among believers. because those who use it hardly ever mean or do what they say. This definitely explains one of the reasons why forgiveness is exhausting. If forgiving did not include the requirement of praying for the offender, a lot more people might be willing to forgive. After all, they could just do it in their hearts at one moment and be done with it. However, the fact that forgiveness is a process that takes time (and serious meditation) means that it is challenging and stressful. In fact, so unfamiliar are some of the requirements for forgiveness that some offended people wonder where to start and end.

As a natural response to the difficulties associated with forgiveness, many people have come up with different versions of what forgiveness means and how it ought to be done. Some claim it is a personal matter that no other person except God has to know about, and others contend that forgiveness is not for people to do but a task to be accomplished by

---

[164] Everett L. Worthington Jr., *Handbook of Forgiveness* (Abingdon, United Kingdom: Routledge, 2007), 27.

God only. This is why when some people are asked to forgive by their offenders, they turn away and claim that it is not for them to forgive but God. All these excuses are an attempt to postpone forgiving or shift the responsibility to forgive from the offender to other people, especially God.

God is the one with the ultimate authority to forgive sins, but he will not come down and help men and women forgive their fellow men and women for the offenses committed against them. Instead, God deliberately asks everyone to forgive those who sin against them. Therefore, offended people have to finish the process of forgiving by, among other things, praying for their offenders.

## Letting Go of Anger and Resentment

A person who has successfully completed the process of forgiveness will also most likely benefit from being able to learn how to manage their anger. Anger, in itself, is not bad because even God gets angry:

> The Lord is compassionate and gracious, slow to anger, abounding in love.[165]

However, anger becomes a problem and a cause for concern when it is held for too long. In this regard, the apostle Paul specifically made the command that people ought not to stay angry for long: "Don't let the sun go down on your wrath."[166]

Unless offended people complete the process of forgiveness, they are at a high risk of experiencing frequent bouts of anger, especially with respect to their offender or when similar offenses are being committed or seem likely to be committed. As noted before, people tend to develop natural defense mechanisms against people and events that are perceived to pose a danger to them.

Unfortunately, one of the ways that offended people may protect themselves from more harm is by becoming overly angry.[167] The anger

---

[165] Psalm 103:8 NIV.

[166] Ephesians 4:26 NIV.

[167] Larry D. Ellis, *Forgiveness: Unleashing a Transformational Process* (Denver, CO: Adoration Publishing Company, 2010), 46.

is supposed to warn others to keep away. Unless an offended person completes the process of forgiveness, pent-up anger may develop and could be directed at other people in general and the offender in particular. This does not mean that the offended person did not intend to forgive. However, forgiveness has to be complete.

When healing does not take place, which happens so many times, offended people become prone to anger. They may become angry at virtually everyone and everything. For instance, they get mad at themselves for having allowed the person to hurt them (or having played a role in the offense). They are angry at the offender for failing to apologize even though the offender was clearly in the wrong. They may be angry at friends for seemingly not understanding their situation. Before long, the person's anger becomes a part of their lives. Healing after forgiving can help the person deal with such anger and avoid destroying their life.

Completing the process of forgiveness also allows offended people not to excuse offenses based on the need to preserve or conserve old or past relationships. This is one of the many fallacies associated with forgiving where offended people are overly inclined to forgive someone or even excuse them because they are a close family member, a church leader, or a fellow brother or sister in the Lord. The reality is that true forgiveness ought not to take into consideration the future of the old or past relationship.[168] This is something for the affected people to decide later. Many offended people rush to forgive in the false assumption that—or in need for—the relationship to be restored. Sometimes they may even be pressured into doing so.

The reality is that forgiveness is only complete when the offended people go through the processes slowly and not in a rushed manner. The slow pace allows them to think about the critical issues, meditate upon them, and get over them with time. A rushed process of forgiveness is best described as a *reconciliation*, and reconciliation in this regard may not necessarily be the same as forgiveness. In fact, it can be argued that it is much easier for two people to get reconciled than to forgive each other. Similarly, reconciliation has often taken the place of forgiveness, and the

---

[168] Robert Jeffress, *When Forgiveness Doesn't Make Sense* (Colorado Springs, CO: WaterBrook, 2000), 47.

two have been used interchangeably. This ought not to be the approach to forgiveness. As was noted before, forgiveness may or may not include the offender and offended people getting reconciled. However, reconciliation is not even part of the process of forgiveness. Therefore, completing the process of forgiveness ensures that offended people do not rush to forgive (or are not rushed to forgive or even get reconciled). Instead, it ensures that they take their time to analyze every critical aspect of the offense from the hurt to the healing.

Many offended people excuse their offenders by saying they did not mean to hurt them. Whether or not the offender intended to hurt becomes insignificant when the process of forgiving begins. While forgiving, the one thing that matters most is the fact that someone was hurt or offended. The magnitude of the offense and the culpability of the offender are less significant considerations, especially at this stage of the forgiveness process. Therefore, the offender may or may not have intended to cause the hurt, but the fact remains that the pain exists anyway. Completing the process of forgiveness enables the offended person to understand that no amount of excusing—or not excusing—the offender can change the fact that he or she was hurt.[169] Subsequently, the person realizes that healing has to follow irrespective of the attitude of the offender.

Moreover, completing the process helps the offended person understand and appreciate that an offense is an offense regardless of who committed it, why, where, and the consequences of the offense. It helps them understand the value of the biblical appeal: "Whoever says to the guilty, 'You are innocent'—people will curse him."[170] When offended people try to minimize the impact of the offense or excuse the offender, it tends to predispose them to more offending and the risk of being hurt against, especially by the same offender. Therefore, completing the process of forgiveness helps the offended person to be more wary of the offender—regardless of the relationship they have—and take necessary measures to protect themselves from possible harm in the future.

---

[169] John F. MacArthur, *The Freedom and Power of Forgiveness*, electronic ed. (Wheaton, IL: Crossway Books, 1998), 24.
[170] Proverbs 24:24 NIV.

## The Need to Avoid Rushed Forgiveness

It is also essential that the offended person completes the process of forgiveness since this helps avoid a rushed decision. When it comes to forgiveness, the tendency is for the offended person to assume that forgiving quickly is enough or amounts to forgiving totally and fully. The temptation to think that forgiving has to follow as soon as the bad experience has taken place is usually overwhelming and should be resisted as much as possible. Many people struggle with this issue, and it is often used to cover up for the hurt or avoid facing the actual facts of the offense. It is relatively easy for the offended person to want to quickly get over and done with the ordeal resulting from the offense to be what they think is free. In reality, such a move is counterproductive because it is a shortcut to total forgiveness. Even if a pardon is ultimately granted, it is only partial or is not genuine. As a result, the offended person will continue to struggle with the offense and the offender. It is unlikely that the hurt and the negative emotions associated with it will disappear.

Unfortunately, there are people who have been trained to forgive quickly and move on as fast as they can. Therefore, they do not waste a moment before they supposedly forgive. As soon as they become aware that someone has hurt them, they quickly conclude that they need to forgive and go ahead and "forgive." After all, they have also been told that forgiveness is in one's heart and that only God can understand what lies deep inside one's heart. Therefore, such people fail to go through the entire process of forgiving. Forgiving as fast as possible is indeed essential. After all, it helps the offended person not to have to bear the burden of bitterness and revenge for a long time. However, this does not mean that it is done without adherence to the due process.

As was noted before, there is no specific formula for forgiving, but the significant steps of phases have to be covered. More often than not, people go through the hurt, hate, and hook phases of the process but leave out the healing period because healing is one of the most challenging operations—and it requires significant time to complete the process. Therefore, completing the process of forgiveness helps the offended person face the full impact of the offense and grieve over whatever happened. People often think grieving is only required for someone who has lost a loved one. Just as a person needs to grieve after losing a loved one, there is also a need to grieve after being hurt by someone. In fact, both the loss of a loved one and being offended by someone—especially someone close—are hurtful events. Sometimes people get deeper hurts through offenses than they do through the loss of loved ones. Some people may think that this is a weird comparison, but it makes a lot of sense.

In fact, it is partly because true forgiveness requires grieving that many people find it challenging to accomplish. Sometimes it has to do with what people think of grieving. Different people have different ways of grieving, and it does not matter how one grieves as long as there is grief. Grieving is a way of dealing with the hurt and releasing any pent-up emotions, such as anger, bitterness, and revenge. Some people cry out loudly, and others shut themselves away for extended periods of time without talking to anyone. The ultimate goal has to be ensuring that the negative emotions associated with the hurt are released. Otherwise, they will negatively affect the person. For instance, not grieving may result in depression after some time. Some people may even have posttraumatic stress disorder as a result of being offended. Therefore, completing the process of forgiveness helps people deal with their emotions, and in doing so, it releases the offender from the bottom of their hearts. This is something that cannot be rushed or forced on anyone. A person cannot force another to grieve over an offense. It is something that comes from within the person and flows out effortlessly and naturally.

Completing the process of forgiveness also helps offended people face the impacts of the offense on them.[171] While different offenses have different results, all offenses have effects that need to be met and accepted or dealt with. These include the consequences of the offense, such as a child being born out of an extramarital affair, losing life savings through theft or fraud, or having to leave a particular church or ministry as a result of having been offended by the pastor or church leaders. As these examples illustrate, one cannot just forgive and move on without having to deal with the consequences of the hurt. If forgiveness is to be completed, the offended person has to face all the impacts of the offense and plan on the

---

[171] John F. MacArthur, *The Freedom and Power of Forgiveness*, electronic ed. (Wheaton, IL: Crossway Books, 1998), 23.

way forward. Sometimes people rush to forgive only to realize later that they cannot live with the impacts. As a result, the bitterness and resentment toward the offender may be restored.

The best approach is to deal with the impacts before forgiving so that everything is taken into consideration before the final decision to forgive is made. Even if a person does not display or manifest anger or resentment after realizing that the impacts of the offense are too much to bear, they may never be able to heal from the offense. Because the effects of sin are mostly felt much later, the process of forgiveness must extend over the period when the impacts are being felt. This way, the offended person can get a feel for just what they are getting into by forgiving. It is better for someone to delay forgiving but then heal completely than to rush to forgive only for the wounds of the offense to remain or emerge every time the impacts of the offense are felt. Therefore, completing the process of forgiveness helps offended people deal with the effects of the offense. This, in turn, helps the person be truthful about their motivations for forgiving.

God is not interested in quick forgiveness if it is not based on genuine feelings. Rather, God "desire[s] truth in the inner parts [and] … teach[es] me wisdom in the inmost place."[172] Forgiveness is difficult when people are not willing to be true to themselves and to their feelings. They pretend they are fine when in fact they are not. They seem to be more concerned about outward appearances and reputations than with the real state of their hearts and how they honestly think and feel about the offender and the offense caused. People may deceive other people—and even deceive themselves—but they can never fool God. He is the Maker, and he searches the inner parts for the truth.

Completing the process of forgiveness helps offended people come to terms with themselves and their feelings about the situation. It helps them realize that this is no easy thing to do—but it has to be done because it is a command and not a suggestion from God to forgive. Forgiving quickly is akin to undermining the real value of forgiveness by making it look simple when it is not. By extension, it is a form of denial and deceit. God is never pleased with people who are deceitful.

---

[172] Psalm 51:6 NIV.

# CONCLUSION

As Jesus Christ breathed his last breath and committed his spirit to the father on that fateful day when he was crucified, it looked like all hope for humankind's redemption had finally come to an end. Those from his family and some of his disciples watched in horror as the man they had come to trust and rely on for virtually every aspect of their lives helplessly hung there on the cross with no way of freeing himself. From their point of view, it was one of the most trying moments of their lives as well as the most challenging time for Jesus Christ. It must have been horrifying to witness the scene unfolding against a backdrop of immense doubt regarding the promises Christ had made about the coming of the kingdom of God. As ordinary human beings made of blood and flesh, they may have wondered about whether this marked the end of the promised kingdom of God or whether there was still hope for them, their loved ones, and all those who would later believe in the Gospel message that Christ had so powerfully proclaimed.

On the other hand, those who crucified Christ were more than convinced that this was the ultimate end of his short-lived reign as King of the Jews. They were sure that nothing could be able to free him from the power of the Roman Empire and the religious leaders who had instigated the entire plan to have Jesus arrested, tried, and crucified for blasphemy. They may have expected Jesus to attempt to rescue himself from the cross as he had done so many times to other people. Therefore, they did all that was humanly possible to offend him and inflict upon him as much pain as they could conceive. It was arguably one of the world's most cruel killings and one that would remain unmatched for years to come.

Even some among those who were closely allied to Jesus chose to part ways with him out of the fear that they would suffer the same fate if they associated themselves with the dying man. In the end, Jesus was all alone on that cross with no one to turn to for help. Even his heavenly Father seemed to have suddenly vanished and he cried out, "Father, Father, why have you forsaken me?" For Jesus to have had such thoughts of being abandoned by his Father, he must have had to endure a lot of pain and suffering. Never before had Jesus even intimated that his Father was a long way from him—let alone leave him entirely. In reality, it is difficult to accurately depict the scene that unfolded that day.

As they taunted him and speared his side, Jesus remained characteristically calm and did not utter a word back at them. Instead, he did not even bother to tell them that they had just crucified the promised Messiah—and that this would not be the end of him. Whatever he knew of himself to be accurate, he kept to himself. This gave his torturers the opportunity and reason to taunt and ridicule him. Some even went as far as asking him to free himself if indeed he was the Son of God or to ask God—his supposed Father—to come to his rescue. Still, Jesus did not say a single word. Instead, he trusted only him who can save everyone from their sinful acts: his heavenly Father. He was reviled, but he said not a word; he was pierced, but he remained as calm as a lamb in the hands of its shearers. He had the power, justification, and opportunity to do whatever he wished, especially in retaliation against his torturers and killers, but he chose not to. This was his attitude at the pint of death just as it had been during his life on earth.

To compound Jesus's problems and misery even at that last hour, one of the two thieves with whom he was being crucified joined in with the other people in ridiculing Jesus and his supposed power. He specifically asked Jesus to free himself and free him as well—if he was the Son of God as he had allegedly claimed. The second thief also joined in, but at least he had some kind words for Jesus. He rebuked his fellow thief, telling him that at least his crucifixion was deserved and justified since he was simply paying for what he had done. However, he said that Jesus's crucifixion was a miscarriage of justice since Jesus had done nothing wrong. At that moment, Jesus told the second thief hanging there beside him that he would be with Jesus in paradise later that day. These are among the few words Jesus spoke as he hung there. However, he also managed to say some more terms that shocked everyone. Jesus prayed to God and asked him to forgive his killers for they knew not what they were doing.

In saying those words, Jesus demonstrated to all those watching and listening that he held nothing against anyone in line with his teachings while on earth. He also made it clear that forgiveness was not only due to those who seek it but to everyone who required to be forgiven regardless of their attitudes. Jesus made it clear that forgiveness was something God demanded of everyone in all circumstances and in spite of all feelings. By forgiving his tormenters even at the very point of death, Jesus demonstrated that while it was not easy for any to forgive, it was mandatory to do so. This command has remained to date in that God expects everyone to forgive those who offend or sin against them—just as God has forgiven sins. However, this does not mean that forgiveness is easy. In fact, forgiveness is one of the most challenging things anyone can ever be asked or required to do. It was against this backdrop that this book explored why it is so difficult to forgive using the Bible as the point of reference. Many people have different reasons why forgiving is difficult, but those views are not necessarily those of God as recorded in the Bible.

The distinction between the Word of God as recorded in the Bible and the views of experts, scholars, theologians, and opinion leaders is vital in this regard because God's Word is always supreme. Moreover, the Word of God has to be obeyed and taken at its face value. God's Word is also flesh because it is written that the Word became flesh and dwelt among people on the earth.[173] By virtue of God's Word being flesh, it is also living and, therefore, actionable. As such, the Word of God is unlike the word of anyone else—regardless of how educated that person might be.

In the same way, there is a major difference between the biblical teachings on forgiveness and what humankind teaches about forgiveness. God's perception of forgiveness is markedly different from how humankind receives forgiveness. It is for this reason that this book sought to explore and understand why forgiveness is so difficult based on the Word of God as recorded in the Bible. After all, biblical truth is absolute, and human truth is relative and variable. Therefore, understanding why it is difficult to forgive has to be commensurate with understanding God's teachings on forgiveness.

---

[173] John 1:1 NIV.

The Bible contains many teachings and lessons on forgiveness, but none of them offer any simple and straightforward answers on why it is so difficult to forgive. It takes a critical analysis and in-depth investigation of the Holy Scriptures to answer this question. In fact, it takes a lot of meditation of the teachings of Christ, the apostles, the prophets, and even the Law of Moses to understand why it is difficult to forgive because forgiveness is a crucial concept across both the Old Testament and the New Testament. It is one of the few practices that were emphasized by both the Law of Moses and Jesus Christ. This emphasis, in turn, points to forgiveness as a practice that God considers to be critical and even indispensable. Forgiveness cannot be dispensed with because it is at the core of Christian practice—just as it was at the center of religious practice during the dispensation of the Law.

This ought not to mean that the requirements for forgiveness remained precisely the same during the New Testament as they were during the dispensation of the Law of Moses. Instead, there have been some interpretational changes. While the core aspects pertaining to forgiveness remained even after the coming and death of Christ, they were interpreted differently because the Law of Moses never made anything perfect. It required "an eye for an eye" and "a tooth for a tooth," but Jesus taught that when a person slaps another on the right cheek, the one being hit ought to let the person slap them on the left cheek as well. In essence, Christ's teachings emphasized the need for offended people to go to great lengths to forgive their offenders while the Law may have adopted a more liberal approach to forgiveness. That is why it is written that the Law was only a shadow of the good things that were to come, being in place only or a limited time until the awaited perfection (through Jesus Christ) became manifest.

Still, the Old Testament provides some of the best answers to why forgiveness is exhausting. The very first act of disobedience against God is recorded in the Old Testament and involved the sin of Adam in the Garden of Eden. When Adam—the first man—sinned against God by disobeying the commands of God, God set forth the process of forgiving. The most important lesson with regard to Adam was not that God forgave him—if God forgave him at all—but that sin has consequences.

The Bible does not exactly say whether God forgave Abraham for the sin he committed, but it makes it clear that Adam was banished from the

Garden of Eden as a result of the sin. Among other lessons, the Adam story teaches shows that forgiveness of sin or offenses is independent of the consequences of the sin. Before God, being forgiven does not mean being set free from the effects of the sin or offense. Instead, sin is dealt with according to what it deserves, regardless of whether there is forgiveness.

From the findings reached and presented in this book, it can be concluded that forgiving is difficult mainly because God's command to forgive effectively goes against human nature, which is to take revenge and pay back evil for evil. This attitude of paying back was also encouraged in the days of the Law of Moses when every sin or offense was repaid in equal measure in what was popularly known as an eye for an eye and a tooth for a tooth. Somehow, this mentality still dominates the thinking of many people long after the old dispensation was replaced by a new one when Christ became the atoning sacrifice for all sins. With Christ's death on the cross, all sins were nailed on the cross, and everyone can now boldly approach the throne of grace with fear to worship God. The blood of bulls and lambs is no longer required as it proved to be insufficient to cleanse those who were guilty of sin thoroughly. Instead, repeated sacrifices is needed. When Christ came, he entered the Holy of Holies and tore down the curtain that separated people from God. He offered the ultimate sacrifice once and for all. Therefore, it is no longer necessary for those who sin to offer sacrifices of blood on a regular basis and every time they have a guilty conscience.

Therefore, people find it difficult to forgive because they find it hard to obey God. That is the bottom line. Their sinful nature has prevented them from walking in the Holy Spirit as God demands of them. It takes a person who walks not by flesh but by the Holy Spirit to realize that forgiving is paramount. Because people walk in the flesh and gratify the evil desires of the flesh, they try to rely on their own power to forgive instead of relying on the power of the Holy Spirit. Without the Holy Spirit, human beings can do nothing. The Holy Spirit is the Guide and the Comforter. Among other things, the Holy Spirit convicts people of their wrongdoings, which enables them to repent of their sins and seek forgiveness. In the same way, the Holy Spirit prompts people to forgive those who have offended in line with God's will. After all, it is only via the Holy Spirit that believers can come to know the will of God.

Because there is nothing that compares to the freedom that comes with forgiving others and being forgiven, Satan is determined to enslave people by hindering their ability to forgive and be forgiven. This way, they can remain in their self-made prisons forever. However, there is still hope. Through the enabling power of the Holy Spirit, everyone can once again overcome the difficulties and forgive those who sin against them. Holding onto unforgiveness only harms the offended person and not the offender, and this alone makes one become a slave to bitterness. With the help of the Holy Spirit, offended people can let go of the bitterness and let God take care of the rest.

It is also difficult to forgive because many people have a misconceived view of forgiveness. These misconceptions are different and vary from one context to another as well as from one person to another. The beliefs that people in one community, ethnicity, or even race hold about forgiveness may be markedly different from that which people from other races, ethnicities, and communities hold about forgiveness. Similarly, it matters a lot whether a person is a believer because faith in Jesus Christ plays a vital role in encouraging people to forgive. This could be because many believers understand that the very state of being a believer is delicate and comes with many challenges.

As Christ rightly put it, those who believe in him are bound to face many challenges in this world on account of their faith. This is not necessarily because they are evil; it is because the one they believe in, Jesus Christ, also faced many challenges and had to endure sufferings, persecutions, and even death on the cross. Therefore, those who believe in Jesus have to expect to experience the same pain and oppression as their Master did. As it is written, those who share in Christ's glory have to also share in his suffering. That is paramount and something every believer has to be prepared for. Being required to forgive is among the problematic yet mandatory challenges that believers have to live with every day. However, believers know that forgiving is a command from God and not a request by him. Therefore, they may be less inclined to forgive those who offend them.

However, even Christians struggle with forgiving. It could be argued that Christians are among those who find forgiveness particularly difficult because they find themselves needing to forgive more often than those who do not believe. Unbelievers, by virtue of not fearing God, often have no problem refusing to forgive those who offend them and even going as far as seeking revenge against their offenders. On the contrary, Christians feel obligated to forgive—even if they have to fabricate it at times. Therefore, forgiving is just as difficult for Christians as it is for non-Christians. However, Christians, in keeping with Christlike character, try to forgive as much as possible. Christians also tend to have better knowledge and understanding of what forgiveness truly entails because they have the firsthand experience of the Word of God and the biblical teachings on forgiveness. This implies that even if they may have some misconceptions about forgiveness, these are fewer compared to unbelievers' misconceptions about forgiveness.

Forgiveness requires a proper understanding of what it truly means to forgive. Most of the time, forgiveness is not what many people think it is or perceive it to be. This, in itself, is a significant hindrance to forgiving. Clearly, it is only to the extent that people charged with doing something understand it correctly that they can do it excellently. Even the most minimal misunderstanding may result in mistakes on the part of those tasked with doing something. The same applies to forgiveness; it is only to the extent that offended people understand what forgiveness means that they are able to forgive. Since everyone needs to forgive and be forgiven, it follows that every human being needs to have a proper understanding of the meaning of forgiveness. Otherwise, they will never "do" it right. As long as misconceptions about forgiveness remain, people will keep finding it hard—or even impossible—to forgive those who offend them.

For instance, many people find it challenging to forgive because they falsely assume that they have to reestablish their past relationships with their offenders. Such people may be more than willing to let go of their resentments and anger toward the offender, but they are not ready to have anything to do with them. Therefore, they refuse to even consider the possibility that they could forgive. Instead, they regard forgiveness as something that will trap them in a relationship, and they find it to be one-sided and unproductive. Rather than risk being trapped in such a relationship, they choose not to forgive, not knowing that forgiveness has nothing to do with reestablishing past relations.

In the same manner, people may refuse to forgive because they falsely believe that forgiving is the same as—or includes—freeing the offender from any responsibilities. This is especially true in offenses where the offended person expects some kind of restitution for the loss suffered or incurred (such as money being repaid or a stolen item being returned). Such people often choose not to forgive because they are concerned that forgiving will cause them to lose whatever the offender took from them or that the offender rightly and justifiably owes them and has to repay or return. Unless whatever is owed is repaid, they may not be willing to explore the possibility of forgiving. If the same people were made aware of the fact that by forgiving, they do not lose their right to be repaid owed debts or obligations, they would not hesitate to repay. This does not apply to the continuing debt of love or to the debt pertaining to forgiveness itself. Forgiveness is a form of debt where the offended people let go of the expectation that their offenders will ever be able to make right the harm or hurt caused to them.

Ultimately, misconceptions about forgiveness—and its meaning—make it difficult for people to forgive. This could explain why the Bible contains so many teachings on what forgiveness entails. One of the most famous passages of scripture in this regard is Jesus's response to Peter's question on the number of times one ought to forgive those who offend others. In his reply, Jesus made it clear that forgiveness needed not to be done only seven times but as many times as possible. In doing so, Jesus effectively demystified a common misconception about forgiveness and one that must have been quite rampant even among Jesus's followers.

For as long as the disciples of Jesus held onto the misconception that forgiveness only needed to be done for a limited period of time, there is reason to believe that they may have been less inclined to forgive. In fact, they could have found forgiveness particularly challenging and difficult because they falsely thought it had to be done only a certain number of times and not always. Moreover, they seemed to believe that they only have to forgive if their offenders sought their apology. While sometimes it becomes imperative that forgiveness be granted because the offender has asked to be forgiven, the reality is that forgiveness has to be independent of the attitude of the offender such that it is given regardless of whether the offender apologizes—or seeks to be forgiven—or is adamant and fails to show any remorse for the offense committed. Therefore, forgiveness is difficult partly because there are so many deep-seated misconceptions about forgiveness that prevent and discourage people from forgiving their offenders.

# BIBLIOGRAPHY

Bash, Anthony. *Forgiveness: A Theology*, vol. 19, Cascade Companions. Eugene, OR: Cascade Books, 2015.

Ellis, Larry D. *Forgiveness: Unleashing a Transformational Process*. Denver, CO: Adoration Publishing Company, 2010.

Fraser Watts and Liz Gulliford, *Forgiveness in Context: Theology and Psychology in Creative Dialogue* (London; New York: T&T Clark, 2004).

Hunt, June. *Biblical Counselling Keys on Forgiveness: The Freedom to Let Go*. Dallas, TX: Hope for The Heart, 2008.

Jeffress, Robert. *When Forgiveness Doesn't Make Sense*. Colorado Springs, CO: Waterbrook, 2000.

MacArthur, John F. *The Freedom and Power of Forgiveness*, electronic ed. Wheaton, IL: Crossway Books, 1998.

McFadyen, Alistair and Marcel Sarot. *Forgiveness and Truth*. Edinburgh; New York: T&T Clark, 2001.

Prince, Derek. *The Three Most Powerful Words: Discovering the Freedom of Releasing the Ones Who Hurt Us*. Charlotte, NC: Derek Prince Ministries, 2006.

Shults, F. LeRon and Steven J. Sandage. *The Faces of Forgiveness: Searching for Wholeness and Salvation*. Grand Rapids, MI: Baker Academic, 2003.

Worthington Jr., Everett L., *Handbook of forgiveness*. Abingdon, United Kingdom: Routledge, 2007.

Zondervan and Zondervan Publishing House. *Holy Bible: New International Version, Textbook Edition*. Grand Rapids, MI: Zondervan, 2011.

# ABOUT THE AUTHOR

Pastor Robert E. Gaines was born on February 23, 1981. He is the younger of two children, born to William T. Gaines and Ruthie L. Gaines. He was educated in the Monroe City School System and graduated from Wossman High School. Upon graduation, he attended Career Technical College.

He continued his education and received his bachelor's degree and his master's degree in theology with honors in both from United Theological Seminary in Monroe, Louisiana. He graduated with his doctoral degree in biblical studies at Louisiana Baptist University and Seminary in Shreveport, Louisiana.

Pastor Robert Gaines has been preaching and teaching the Word of God for more than eighteen years. He began to serve faithfully at the St. Joe Missionary Baptist Church in Rhymes, Louisiana, as an associate minister, Sunday school teacher, and choir member. He delivers the Word of God through preaching and teaching, and he is an aspiring gospel artist who ministers through his gift of singing.

Currently, he proudly serves as the senior pastor of the St. Mark Missionary Baptist Church in Bonita, Louisiana, and he celebrated ten years of pastoring God's flock in October 2019. He has incorporated a vision statement—A loving, learning, and living fellowship united to proclaim the Gospel, perfect the saint, and promote unity in the Body of Christ—as the foundation to the ministry he sets forth. During his tenure as pastor, St. Mark has experienced tremendous growth. The membership has increased substantially, the spiritual climate continues to escalate, and the congregation is known as a loving family striving to live in God's will for their lives. Pastor Gaines has led the group in establishing several new ministries. The impact of Pastor Gaines's teaching and preaching can be heard online during his live stream every second, fourth, and fifth Sunday at 11:00 a.m. For all of the above, Pastor Gaines gives God complete glory!